IN THE SAME SERIES

MASTERS OF MUSIC:
Purcell to Liszt.   By Sydney Grew.

ROMANCE OF THE PIANO.
By Eric Blom.

THE LUTE PLAYER

by

CARRAVAGGIO

MAKERS OF MUSIC

MUSIC

THE STORY OF SINGERS AND INSTRUMENTALISTS

BY

SYDNEY GREW

LONDON

G. T. FOULIS & CO. LTD.

MILFORD LANE, W.C.2

PRINTED IN GREAT BRITAIN BY
MORRISON AND GIBB LTD., LONDON AND EDINBURGH

INTRODUCTION

by Sir Landon Ronald

THE author of this book sets out to tell the story of some of the great performers of music for voice, piano and violin. This is an interesting story, not often told except in books dealing with one great virtuoso at a time. More or less incidentally, it tells at the same time the history of the rise and development of their three departments of musical art, which began and, for a long time, continued with the work of performers who were also composers—though not composers who have to be reckoned among the Masters.

I am naturally delighted to stand sponsor for such a book, being myself the director and overseer of the work of many hundreds of young musicians whose purpose in life is to become performers, and having had myself many years of experience before the public as a Conductor.

The importance of the interpretative artist is not always fully recognized, nor is the influence of the fine executive virtuoso upon the great composers altogether fully realized. We know, of course, that without performance music is inclined to be rather a lifeless thing, but we do not all know that the performers are co-creators with the composers, serving to complete the expression of their ideas. Still less do we all know that, in most cases, the virtuosos precede the composer as well as follow him, showing

I

INTRODUCTION

him what is possible of execution, and in many instances (and I have no doubt of this) inspiring him much as afterwards they inspire an audience to a complete appreciation of his music.

History books in general cannot offer you what Mr. Sydney Grew provides in such a book as this, and that is the real human side of those fine performers who, by their technical and imaginative qualities, made possible the work of the Masters. This is because the history books have too many other matters to attend to. Yet the enforced omission is a pity, for not only are the performers men and women of delightful, charming and often amusing character, but they are also essential elements of history, without knowledge of whom our education is incomplete and whose absence from the records renders history the rather dry thing most young students find it.

The more we realize that all musicians of the past, whatever their position, were at heart simply human beings, even as we of to-day are the same, the better fitted we are to understand music and to make it ourselves in performance. We should never lose sight of the human qualities of our art ; when performing music we must strive to feel ourselves a living link between the audience, with its varied interests, and the humanity as well as the art of the composer. That is the attitude adopted by Mr. Grew in this book, and it is that which should make it

2

INTRODUCTION

exceptionally acceptable and interesting to students, artists and all those interested in music alike.

I can only repeat in conclusion that I am proud to be its sponsor.

LANDON RONALD

Several chapters of this book are reprinted from *The Strad* and *Musical Opinion*. The poem (by Eva Mary Grew) which appears on pages 18-19 is also reprinted from *The Strad*.

CONTENTS

I. VIOLINISTS

II. PIANISTS

CONTENTS

III. SINGERS

ILLUSTRATIONS

I. VIOLINISTS

To MAX MOSSEL

I. INTRODUCTORY

THE violinist, more than the player of any other instrument, and more even than the singer, has the curious power to disturb minor poets, and writers of emotional prose, and to set them expressing themselves in terms of easy sentimentality and extravagance. An illustration of this truth was given in the present writer's *Favourite Musical Performers*, where on page 231, in the chapter on Albert Sammons, a quotation is made from a contemporary article on Kubelik and his debut. That Kubelik article could be cited as one of a string running from the first violinist of note to the last, for the habit repeats itself ; or rather, it is self-generated every season.

There is nothing unnatural here. The elementary qualities in the art of the violin are at once apparent, and their effect on the minor poet is immediate ; these qualities do not go beyond melody, and are not confused (for the minor poet) by harmony and grand form. All that the violinist does is visible, and his creations are not hampered by words and intellectual ideas, as are the creations of the singers ; and what the minor poet sees is what he can speak of. Then again, there are two kinds of violinist—one of the classical, who plays as Bach and Beethoven write, the other of the romantic or virtuosic, whose mind and work are (relatively to Bach and Beethoven's) child-like, and who appeals with force to the minor poet and to that

11

vast multitude of simple music-lovers of whom he is the direct representative and spokesman.

The virtuoso (sometimes called trickster, showman, and charlatan—Paganini being the supreme example) throws his audience into a state of excitement by his wonderful pianola-like technique and by his faculty of imitating natural sounds : out of this excitement comes the minor poem ; and so where we have a hundred good poems of this minor class, we have only one—if we have one at all—which tells of the influence of the classical performer. The excitement that comes of the work of the latter is deep, rare and wellnigh inexpressible, except by a poet like Browning. There are scores of poems addressed to Paganini, Ole Bull, Sarasate, and others of the same kind, and very few addressed to Joachim, Ysaye and Kreisler.

The following pages contain an account of the rise of the classical school of violin playing, from its formation by Corelli to its development in the first part of the nineteenth century, when the great Parisian players were at work and Spohr was active in Germany.

At the same time, a full enough account is given of the various individual virtuosos who lived their lives and did their work side by side with the members of the classical school. Indeed, my story closes with two of these individual virtuosos—Paganini and Ole Bull ; because

INTRODUCTORY

all the later masters of the classical style can be readily understood by the young reader out of his or her general knowledge of the school to which they belong.

The virtuosos are harder to understand, because they are always individuals—men almost entirely *sui generis*, springing from no uniform body of artists, and leaving no progeny.

Before describing the course of this art, I recommend you to observe the mood and manner of the following poems, so that the general attitude of the world to violinists shall be clear to you. We are all likely to have some interfering fancy or predilection, or to be influenced by a general prejudice ; and this must always be removed when we set out to observe history.

Leigh Hunt wrote a long poem about Paganini. He was an unblushing Cockney gusher on such a subject, and this is his portrait of the performer :

> The exceeding mystery of the loveliness
> Sadden'd delight ; and with his mournful look,
> Dreary and gaunt, hanging his pallid face
> 'Twixt his dark flowing locks, he almost seem'd
> To feeble or to melancholy eyes,
> One that had parted with his soul for pride,
> And in the sable secret liv'd forlorn.

The player has a " full and trembling fervour " ; he has " thoughts finer than hope " : and he raises

MAKERS OF MUSIC

a pray'r
So earnest vehement, yet so lowly sad,
Mighty with want and all poor human tears,
That never saint, wrestling with earthly love,
And in mid-age unable to get free,
Tore down from heav'n such pity.

And then, out of his despair,

Jump would he into some strange wail uncouth
Of witches' dance, ghastly with whinings thin
And palsied nods—mirth wicked, sad, and weak.

Paganini did all this ; the point to observe is
that his actions are approved of.   More—

you should hear
His instrument become a tree far off,
A nest of birds and sunbeams, sparkling both,
A cottage bow'r ; or he would condescend,
In playful wisdom which knows no contempt,
To bring to laughing mem'ry, plain as sight,
A farm-yard with its inmates, ox and lamb,
The whistle and the whip, with feeding hens
In household fidget muttering evermore,
And, rising as in scorn, crown'd chanticleer,
Ordaining silence with his sovereign crow. . . .

Until

The thunder of th' uprolling house came down,
And bow'd the breathing sorcerer into smiles.

This is about as bad as the matter can be ;
but it shows the simple mind of a true worshipper

INTRODUCTORY

of the virtuoso. Leigh Hunt would have listened earnestly to Joachim playing Bach ; but the poem he might have written on that subject would have been as bad as Paganini's rendering of the same Bach might have been.

Sarasate was a genuine musician, trained in the great Parisian school, and gifted with the mind to interpret all the great music of the world, except that of Bach. That is to say, he was not of the Paganini type. But the minor poet, going to him with the feeble wonder of the Paganini audience, reduces him to that type ; and so Eric Mackay writes of him as follows :

> See how he bends to greet his soul's desire,
> His violin, which trembles like a lyre,
> And seems to trust him, and to know his touch,
> Belov'd so much.
>
> And who can doubt the right it has to lie
> So near his heart, and there to sob and sigh,
> And there to shake its octaves* into notes
> With bird-like throats.
>
> A thousand heads are turn'd to where he stands,
> A thousand hopes are moulded to his hands,
> And, like a storm-wind hurrying from the north,
> A shout breaks forth.
>
> It is the welcome that of old was given
> To Paganini ere he join'd in Heaven
> The angel-choirs of those who serve aright
> The God of Light

*Writers uneducated in music attach a special meaning to " octaves " which musicians have not yet discovered.

MAKERS OF MUSIC

It is the large, loud utterance of a throng
That loves a faith-employ'd, impassion'd song ;
A song that soothes the heart, and makes us sad,—
                    Yet keeps us glad

For look ! how bearded men and women fair
Shed tears, and smile, and half repeat a prayer,
And half are shamed in their so mean estate,
                    And he so great.

The shouts, the praises, and the swift acclaim,
That men have brought to magnify thy name,
Affect thee barely as an idle cheer
                    Affect a seer. .

There is much more of the poem, of which
nearly a hundred thousand copies have been
purchased.

Longfellow, being a true poet, could touch
on music without being ridiculous. His images
might often be flat, but they are never false to
sense, like that of Mackay when he calls
Sarasate's violin a May-day bird that trills without
a tongue. And so Longfellow's poem on Ole
Bull, the perfect Norse musician, as Sarasate,
in different measure, was the perfect Spanish
musician, shows us the true substance of his
violinist's art and proves that the listener understood the subject. I can copy only a few lines ;
and we must not forget that Longfellow happened
to be in warm intellectual sympathy with
Scandinavian poetry :

INTRODUCTORY

He lived in that ideal world
Whose language is not speech, but song ,
Around him evermore the throng
Of elves and sprites their dances whirled ;
The Strömkarl sang, the cataract hurled
Its headlong waters from the height ;—
And mingled in the wild delight
The scream of sea-birds in their flight,
The rumour of the forest trees,
The plunge of the implacable seas
The tumult of the wind at night,
Voices of eld, like trumpets blowing,
Old ballads and wild melodies
Through mist and darkness pouring forth,
Like Elivagar's river flowing
Out of the glaciers of the North . .

The attitude sustained by Leigh Hunt and
Eric Mackay is that which I would ask young
musicians not to adopt. That of Longfellow
is more true, and therefore more dignified and
helpful, to ourselves, music, and the performer.
It enables us to go so far as to declare the great
classical performer a worthy companion of the
great classical composer :

Belov'd of all to whom that Muse is dear
Who hid her spirit of rapture from the Greek,
Whereby our art excelleth the antique,
Perfecting formal beauty to the ear ;
Thou that hast been in England many a year
The interpreter who left us naught to seek,
Making Beethoven's inmost passion speak,
Bringing the soul of great Sebastian near.
    Their music liveth ever, and 'tis just
That thou, good Joachim, so high thy skill,

MAKERS OF MUSIC

Rank (as thou shalt upon the heavenly hill)
Laurel'd with them, for thy ennobling trust,
Remember'd when thy loving hand is still
And every ear that heard thee stopt with dust.

In this manner Robert Bridges addresses
Joseph Joachim, at the same time stating the
very nature of music and showing how, in the
modern world, music takes the place of the
plastic arts that flourished in the ancient world.
Such an attitude enables us even to wr te verse
to express our own convictions and feelings,
because it is creatively personal, and therefore
the most profitable of all attitudes :

Heaven's thought and joy didst thou create,
So easy, simple, and yet how great !
In tones that seemed not made by hand.
Thy bow, like to a celestial wand
Down-drawn from Heaven to Earth, did prove
The spell of music, and deeply move
Our souls anew, inspire, and lift.
Thou, ministering with thy rarest gift,
Knowest well thyself the instrument
Of God, ambassador from Him sent,—
A High Priest, set before His altars,
Whose grave, ennobling air ne'er falters ;
And, as in holy places, we partake
With thee, our spirits to remake,
O noble mind ! what earnestness
Was mixed with thy intent to bless!

'Neath ardent, heavy-lidded eyes,

INTRODUCTORY

Inscrutable, and sad, yet wise,
You sang the masters' melodies;
Passing all through your master-hand,
Beethoven you made us understand
Clear as Corelli or Mozart;
Handel, Bach, Franck, all in their part
Newly created did appear,—
With loving insight brought more near.
Your mingled passion and quietude
Gave life to men's dull platitude,—
'Tis excellent bowing—left-hand good—
The latest fiddlers yet withstood!

Long after your last note was played
Your audience lingered, would have stayed,
Enthralled by your fine manly strength.
The rapt applause ceasing at length,
I heard a voice beside me say,
" Know ye that God was here to-day,
Bringing the joy and thought of Heaven
To ease the sorrow Earth hath given."

These lines (by Eva Mary Grew) are addressed to Kreisler.

II. BEFORE CORELLI

Violins, and consequently violin-playing, have a history that goes back over six or seven hundred years.

But the instrument did not arrive at its present shape much earlier than the middle of the sixteenth century, and the first complete master of the principles of playing did not appear until Corelli, who died in 1713. Moreover, this Italian did not discover those principles and elements of performance which on the one side are " virtuosic " and on the other " dramatic " ; that is to say, he and his music were not brilliant in the Liszt pianoforte manner or intensely poetical in the manner of Beethoven, Schumann and Chopin.

Therefore, although Corelli laid the foundations of violin playing, erecting on those foundations an art which is still alive, the modern art—which we have to-day in Kreisler, Ysaye, Heifetz, Elman, Vecsey, Zimbalist, Kubelik and others—is of still later growth than his period.

And so we can consider that violin playing arose a hundred years after singing, just as we can consider that piano playing arose a hundred years after violin playing.

The making of violins was at its greatest in the period when the playing of violins became virtuosic—as is always the case in the matter of musical instruments, the maker and the per-

BEFORE CORELLI

former inspiring and reacting upon one another. This was around the year 1700. Among the performers were Vivaldi, Veracini and Tartini, and among the makers were the families of the Amati, Guarneri and Stradivari. The latter all lived in Northern Italy and in the Tyrol ; their profession was a family tradition, followed by several generations in succession, and culminating in one supreme craftsman.

The direct cause of the rise of violin playing was the change that came over music at the end of the seventeenth century. The new music is called Monodic, in order to distinguish it from the earlier mediæval music which is called Polyphonic. The solo voice and the violin are monodic instruments.

Opera and the *bel canto* kind of vocal music developed rapidly ; the melodic music of the violin developed slowly. The reason of this lies in the nature of music.

Music is either descriptive or serious and reflective. That is, it is either poetically impassioned, and associated with verbal text or stage action ; or it is " pure." Naturally the help of poetry, action and narrative caused the dramatic kind to develop quickly, and this speed was quickened still more by the fact that the human voice was an already perfected instrument. Art becomes reflective or pure only when its general nature is thoroughly understood, which is never until it has passed away from such an associative condition as music in song or opera.

Classical violin music, and the classical style of playing, are reflective, in the manner just defined.

Moreover, there was, as there always has been, a bigger demand for opera and singing than for violin music, and a branch of art develops according to its audience and to the number of its executants. A thousand good singers are born to one good instrumentalist ; and probably a hundred good operas have been made to one good violin sonata or concerto.

Yet when violin playing was once safely established, it immediately caught up with singing. Tartini played quite as well as Farinelli sang. And having come abreast of its companion, it quickly surpassed it, so that Kreisler to-day plays better than Tetrazzini sings. This also is in the nature of things : the human voice cannot be improved on ; as it was in 1600, so it is to-day, while music has gone on into a world the earlier masters of modern music could not have dreamed of. The violin since the time of Haydn and Mozart has been the mainstay of music ; and despite the development of instrumentation since the time of Beethoven, it must remain its mainstay. But truly great solo players remain rare, not more than fifty or sixty appearing in history.

BEFORE CORELLI

II

For nearly two hundred years the chief composers of music were violinists. Then for another hundred years they were pianists. Now they rarely play any instrument with exceptional skill, because creative labour is greater and more taxing to-day than formerly.

The first writers of music for the violin were themselves performers on the viol, who used the *little viol*, or viol-in, for special purposes, and probably with no idea that it was to become the chief of the stringed instruments played with a bow. Their names—as the names of Paolo Quagliati and Biagio Marini—are without life ; and what remains of their music is valueless.*
Monteverde, one of the greatest violists of the time, and the first writer of true operas, invented for his *Combattimento del Tancred e Clorinda* 1624) the tremolo and the pizzicato.† The players in his orchestra could not produce these effects ; they declared them impossibilities, and probably laughed at the idea at rehearsal ; until Monteverde took up his violin and showed them the way, upon which they would be delighted

---

* I do not give other names in the text, because they would only convey to the page a dull air of learning ; but the student wishing to observe this particular matter more fully may look up the dictionary accounts of Tarquinio Merula, Giovanni Battista Fontana, Mont' Albano, Paolo Ucellini, Massimiliano Neri, and other minor Italian musicians who lived between 1600 and 1650.

† See my *The Origin of Opera, and other Essays on Music.*

with the novelty and show it to all who would listen.

The theatre, however, was not the place where the art of violin playing could come to its own, for in the theatre the instrument was but a support and decorative accompaniment. Its proper place was the music-chamber of kings and nobles, and the church—especially the church, where music for stringed instruments was played at the end of the service.

Composers soon invented the sonata and the concerto, which were forms peculiarly suited to the violin. This was not the sonata of Haydn, Mozart and Beethoven, but the sonata of Bach and Handel. It was of two kinds. One, the Chamber Sonata, or *sonata da camera*, contained dance movements ; the other, the Church Sonata, or *sonata da chiesa*, had no dance rhythms, but was grave, stately, and intellectual in the manner of the fugue.

The latter gradually ousted the former in Italy. Its quiet, thoughtful and restrained manner went to the making of the classical style of Italian violin music ; which was good at first, though eventually it proved a hindrance to the rapid development in that country of the genuine violin style.

Here we have the clue to the first hundred years in the history of this art. It was essentially dignified, both in music and in performance, with no rapturous personal warmth, no abandon to mood, and no animated vigour. Its melodies were sustained, and gracefully figured ; and its quick passages were clearly articulated. This criticism applies even to the music of Purcell.

III

Among the best masters of this epoch was Giovanni Battista Vitali (born about 1644, died in 1692). He wrote a vast quantity of music, of which we ocasionally hear a sonata to-day. It is believed that Vitali influenced Purcell, because Nicolo Matteis, an Italian who visited England, would for certain bring with him some of Vitali's works, together with the works of other Italian composers—Bassani, G. M. Bononcini and the mysterious Lelio Calista, whom Purcell mentions in his edition of Playford's " Introduction to the Skill of Musick."

The Italian players went into all the other European countries. As far back as 1626, which was fifty years before the time of Matteis and Purcell, Carlo Farina had joined the court musicians of the King of Saxony, living inDresden. This Farina was the first Paganini in history, in the respect that he amused his listeners with farm-yard effects. Otherwise he wrote airs, dances and pot-pourris (" quodlibets ").

French players were not of much account until well on in the eighteenth century. As late as 1750 they thought Corelli's music difficult.

MAKERS OF MUSIC

When at last the French found themselves here, they advanced rapidly and around 1800 were the finest performers in Europe.

Nor were German players of much account until the middle of the eighteenth century. The centre of the finest violin playing was Dresden ; yet even in Dresden the German musicians of Corelli's time were far below him. Johann Jacob Walther, a Thuringian, born about 1650, had a good technique ; but musically he was of the Paganini type, using his instrument to imitate birds, flutes, trumpets and other external sounds. One German musician, a Bohemian named Heinrich Biber (1644-1704), was grave and serious in the Italian way, and at the same time warmly poetical in the German. Biber was a man to respect. The Austrian emperor thought highly of him, granting him a patent of nobility. Bohemian, Austrian, Hungarian and German musicians are all called German in the early history of modern music.

IV

Germans, as well as Italians, travelled to other countries. One of them, a native of Lübeck, by name Thomas Baltzar, who was born about the year 1630, came here in Cromwell's time, where his technical ability excited a good deal of attention. He was the first clever performer heard in England.

BEFORE CORELLI

The writer from whom we get most of our knowledge of Baltzar is Anthony Wood (1632-1695), the Oxford antiquarian, music-lover and bell-ringer. Wood taught himself to play, tuning the strings in fourths, and picking out any song he had heard two or three times. He had lessons from a Charles Griffiths, " whom he then thought to be a most excellent artist." Later on, Anthony " entertained one William James, a dancing master, to instruct him on the violin, who by some was accounted excellent on the instrument, and the rather, because it was said that he had obtained his knowledge of dancing and music in France." But Anthony Wood found that these men, Griffiths and James, were not " complete masters of their faculty . . . and to say the truth, there was no complete master in Oxon for that instrument, because it had not been hitherto used in consort among gentlemen. only by common musitians, who played but two parts."

The gentlemen still played the viols, in four and five parts, as they continued to do till Charles II came back and established, on the French plan, his band of twenty-four violins.

Wood met Baltzar in 1658, and he thus tells the story of his first hearing " the Swede " play the violin. " Tho. Baltzar, a Lubecker borne, and the most famous artist for the violin that the world had yet produced, was now in Oxon, and this day, July 24 [1658] A. W. was with him

27

and Mr. Ed. Low, lately organist of Christ Church, at the house of Will. Ellis. A. W. did then and there, to his very great astonishment, heare him play on the violin. He then saw him run up his fingers to the end of the finger-board of the violin, and run them back insensibly, and all with alacrity and in very good tune, which he nor any in England saw the like before. A. W. entertained him and Mr. Low with what the house could then afford, and afterwards he invited them to the taverne ; but they being engaged to goe to other company, he could no more heare him play or see him play at that time. Afterwards he came to one of the weekly meetings at Mr. Ellis's house, and he played to the wonder of all the auditory ; and exercising his finger and instrument several ways to the utmost of his power ; Wilson thereupon, the public professor, the greatest judge of musick that ever was, did, after his humoursome way, stoop downe to Baltzar's feet, to see whether he had a huff on, that is to say, to see whether he was a devil or not, because he acted beyond the parts of man."

All specially astonishing players were suspected (seriously, not, as here, " humoursomely ") of being in league with the devil ; the rumours were worth money, as Paganini found nearly two hundred years later.

There was another meeting, in which A. W. was forced to show his skill by the side of Baltzar's. Present at the " consort " was Mr

BEFORE CORELLI

Davis Mell, a London clockmaker, " accounted hitherto the best for the violin in England ; but after Baltzar came to England, and shewed his most wonderful parts on that instrument, Mell was not so admired, yet he played sweeter [than the German], was a well-bred gentleman, and not given to excessive drinking as Baltzar was."

Poor foolish Baltzar was made head of the king's band of violins ; but " being much beloved by all the lovers of Musick, his company was therefore desired : and company, especially musical company, delighting in drinking, made him drink more than ordinary, which brought him to his grave." He died in 1663, not more than thirty-three years old, and ten years after the birth of Corelli.

III. CORELLI

ALL the diverse activities of the violin during the seventeenth century were summed up in the art of Arcangelo Corelli and brought to unity, excepting only the farm-yard effects and similar imitations.

He was an artist of the exalted kind, whose desire was to serve pure music ; and it was by accepting all the good and throwing out all the bad that he brought violin music to this synthetic condition. Such men as he have no interest in what startles us by its unexpectedness, because the unexpected has no place in the permanencies of art. He had his defects and deficiencies, of course, since the slang of art often betokens a lively imagination which, when absent from the purist, is a rather serious lack ; but for a hundred years his works were the most popular of all in the concert-room ; his great successor, Tartini, looked on them as essential in the study of violin playing ; and few players, even to-day, do not work at the best of them. This is a high record, especially for a man born less than fifty years after the art was first shaped.

I

He was born in 1653, five years before Purcell, and thirty years before Domenico Scarlatti, the first musician to discover a new style for playing keyed instruments.

It is said that his master was Giovanni Battista

30

CORELLI

CORELLI

Bassani, a man whose fame almost equalled Corelli's, so that an English poet, complimenting Purcell, could say :

> In thy productions we, with wonder, find
> Bassani's genius with Corelli's joined.

Bassani was a good musician in the manner of his time, which was a manner gentle rather than robust. But he was four years younger than Corelli ; and though Corelli was not of the kind to develop rapidly and early, being nothing of a child prodigy, none the less he was scarcely of the kind to develop so slowly that his master could be a man younger than himself.

Corelli is understood to have visited Paris in 1672. They say his fame and skill were notable enough to move the jealousy of Lully, the master musician of the city. In this year Bassani was fifteen years old. He is also understood to have gone into Germany about the year 1680, spending some of his time there in the court band of the King of Bavaria and the rest of it with Farinelli, the violinist, the uncle of the singer and composer of that famous piece known as *Farinel's Ground*. We know little of his early life, however.

Soon after 1681 he settled himself in Rome, in the household of the great Cardinal Ottoboni. Here Corelli remained for the rest of his life, rising quickly to the highest musical position in the city, and winning that European fame which

31

c

is intimated in the couplet quoted a few lines back. He taught a good deal ; and it became fashionable in the young men visiting Italy from France, Germany and England, to have a few lessons from Corelli, if music was their pleasure. His chief official duty in the cardinal's palace was to organize the Monday evening concerts and to lead the band.

Corelli's first set of sonatas was published when he was thirty. The solo pieces on which his fame chiefly rests, and which have done so much to stabilize the art of violin playing, were not published until he was nearly fifty.

This great man's technique was in no way phenomenal, but indeed little more than simple. He went to the third position only, and his figurations are not virtuosic. Thus early in the eighteenth century he began to be left behind as an executant. Younger men surpassed him, and the world of impatient youth that crowded around him added to his pain and confusion ; for he was a mild person, very gentle and quiet.

The story is familiar of his inability to play a passage in a work of Handel's which was produced in Rome when the " divine Saxon " was there on his Italian visit of 1706-1710 : Handel explained how the passage was to be performed, and at last he took the violin out of Corelli's hands and dashed through it ; whereupon Corelli said, " But, dear Saxon, this music is in the French style, of which I have no ex-

perience." Visiting Naples in 1708, he was
put out by the King declaring his slow music
to be tedious and leaving the room ; he was so
put out that later in the concert he twice made the
mistake of beginning in the major a piece written
in the minor : these experiences distressed him ;
he felt he had disgraced himself, and slipped away
secretly to Rome. Then when he reached Rome,
he found that during his short absence the people
there had become infatuated with a couple of
showy musicians, of the type he had always
despised and detested.

Corelli therefore withdrew from public life.
He was now fifty-five years old ; his life's work
was finished, and he died in 1713.

II

He had saved six thousand pounds. This was
an achievement, because in those days a violinist
was not a singer, able to command a hundred
pounds fee for appearing at a concert ; nor was
he as a Paganini, who often gained a thousand
pounds. Certainly, Corelli was a man careful
of money ; he wore dark clothes—blue, or black,
because they lasted longer without cleaning,
and he would never hire a coach if his destination
were within walking distance : indeed, he always
went on foot while in the city. Yet even so,
six thousand pounds means that, comparatively,
he earned much money by his profession. More-

over, he left a good collection of valuable pictures, painting being his love apart from music ; though the majority of these he had secured at a cheap rate through his acquaintances among the Italian artists.

Unhappily for our wish to admire Corelli, he left all his possessions to the cardinal. This proves that he was a watch-penny and money-lover. Such men do not like to think that what they have so painstakingly gathered together is to be scattered abroad the moment it has passed out of their control, and they would rather their mite went to swell some larger hoard. Only for this reason could the musician have dropped his little offering into the vast running stream of the churchman's wealth.

However, Ottoboni remembered Corelli's poor relations and gave them the money. But he kept the pictures. We shall see in due course that Tartini, a different man from Corelli in this matter of money, acted very differently indeed.

III

So long as any of Corelli's pupils remained alive in Rome, the master was honoured by a yearly memorial performance of his works. A wealthy admirer, aided by the cardinal, placed a marble bust over his grave. His favourite violin was brought to England by a man named Corbet, from whom it passed to another man who

CORELLI

lived in Newcastle. When this second owner
died, the instrument was bought by Charles
Avison, the Newcastle organist of whom you may
read in Browning's great poem ; and in due
course of time Avison gave it to Giardini.

Geminiani, one of the Italian violinists (Giardini
was another) who lived in England, said that the
violin in Corelli's hands sounded like a sweet
trumpet. He played with a firm tone, all the
notes very even ; and it was commented on
as an original feature that all the violinists in a
band under his direction bowed in the same way,
which means that under other directors each
man bowed as he chose, up or down regardless
of his companions, and with very rough results.

We must realize that Corelli did not write or
play with passion, and that he had not a big,
impetuous nature. We shall then understand
how he could, at this early date, clarify and
stabilize the art of his instrument. If his individuality had been poetically powerful, it would
have driven him into another path, and he could
not then have observed, reflected, tested, and
composed in the manner necessary in the carrying
out of his life's mission. Imagine a warm-blooded
virtuoso in the place of Corelli, and you see the
founding of true violin playing delayed another
generation.

His work made possible bold developments,
even while he was yet alive, because it provided
the universal sub-structure on which men might

35

build freely. It was admired by all musicians, and his music became " classical " before he died : " men remembered, and would refer to, passages in it as to a classic author," says the historian Hawkins. No other composer's pieces were so regularly played in the concert room for the half-century following his death ; and when old Joseph Corfe, who died in 1820, wrote his textbook of Thorough-Bass, he drew nine-tenths of his examples of harmony from Corelli—which, however, was by then rather an old-fashioned proceeding.

To-day we occasionally hear in public one of the sonatas, or that piece which, entitled *Folies d'Espagne*, is based on Farinel's Ground. The true Corelli, with the full measure of vigour that was his, is indicated in the following theme

This is the subject of the double fugue in the fourth of the Twelve Sacred Sonatas. The fugue runs to thirty-nine bars. Sebastian Bach, as part of his studies in Italian music, took this dual subject and wrote on it a fugue for the organ, of which the length is a hundred and two bars.

CORELLI

Two great lines of players spring from Corelli and Tartini. These meet in one man—Pugnani —and then spread into a hundred streams.

Corelli had for pupil Giovanni Battista Somis (1676-1763), among whose pupils were Geminiani (already mentioned), Giardini (also already mentioned), and Pugnani. The last-named, Pugnani, studied under Tartini as well as under Somis.

The great Viotti had Pugnani for master ; and among Viotti's pupils were Robberechts from whom comes Ysaye, by the intermediary stages of De Bériot and Vieuxtemps), Rode (who, by Böhm, Joachim, Hubay, reaches down to von Vecsey), and Baillot (whose pupils in the second and third generations include Sarasate, Jacques Thibaud, Sainton and César Thomson).

The reader need not try to remember the contents of the above paragraph ; but he may profitably refer to it while reading the pages that follow, until these lines and groups of players are as clear to him as the groups of the great composers of music.

IV. VIVALDI AND VERACINI

WHEN a branch of art comes to the climax to which is afterwards given the name Classical, a disturbance immediately follows, and for a time the calm and strength of the art appear to be shattered.

The shattering is necessary, because nothing more can be done on the old lines until some new ideas and practices are formed and brought into the art. The men who remain of the old classical turn of mind are smaller than the master who has effected the climax ; they can only work imitatively, and art will not live by imitation, but by creation alone.

The men of the new turn of mind are also smaller, though during their lifetime they seem bigger, since they loom more prominently and attract more attention by the fine energy and astonishing novelty of their work. These new men proceed by an acceptance of what the classical master rejected, or they lift to a supreme place in their work certain elements which, in his, had but a minor place.

As a rule, the new man, being iconoclastic, has but a slighting regard for the classic ; he and his followers truly believe that it is worn out and that the sun shines nowhere except on them : if they were without this belief, they would be unable to do their new work.

Sometimes, indeed, the classical art is completely submerged for a time, for the reason that it means nothing to the generation of the new men, their minds being so different, and their desires in art so powerfully individual. But sooner or later it comes forward again, and then we have a " revival."

The violinists of the Corellian school fell into dullness. The works of the master lived ; but the works of his exact followers were dead in their birth. The second great master among the Italians, Tartini, built his art on Corelli ; but the chief of the Italian violinists between Corelli and Tartini were vigorously independent. Of the latter I shall here speak of two only, their names standing at the head of this section of my essay.

1

Don Antonio Vivaldi was born about 1675. This was twenty years later than Corelli, and twenty years earlier than Tartini. He died in 1743.

His art, both of composing and of playing, incorporated all that the Roman classical school rejected. He strove to interest, startle and surprise, and aimed to be a popular virtuoso of the violin in the way Farinelli and the rest were popular virtuosos of the voice. Yet Vivaldi was a good musician : he understood form well— as indeed did all the Italians up to a certain point, beyond which they did not go, lacking the emotional power and spiritual ideality of the Germans. He wrote many concertos for violin and accompanying instruments (the concerto having been "invented" by the composer, Giuseppe Torelli, *c.* 1660-1708).

Few players of the time could execute all the minute figurations he wrote in his music. "If acute and rapid notes are evils," says Burney, "Vivaldi has much of the sin to answer for." His farm-yard music (I do not use this term altogether disparagingly, but as a more vigorous expression, and without doubt a more exact expression, than the other terms, pictorial, programmic and imitative) was very popular : "During my youth," Burney tells us, "the *Cuckoo Concerto* was the wonder and delight of all frequenters of country concerts ; and Woodcock, one of the Hereford waits [quite appropriately named] was sent for far and near to perform it."

Burney further says that the solo pieces of Vivaldi which were called *Stravaganze* "occupied the highest place of favour among flashy players, whose chief merit was rapid execution." Some of his concertos "are a pretended paraphrase, in musical notes, of so many sonnets on the four seasons, wherein the author endeavours, by the force of harmony, and particular modifications of air and measure, to excite ideas correspondent with the sentiments of the several poems. . . . The plan of this work must appear very ridiculous," writes the other historian of the eighteenth century, Hawkins.

Hawkins, like all contemporary critics, has

no good word for Vivaldi, who—·in the words of an English traveller in Italy—" was a topping man among them [the priest-musicians] at Venice."

There is, however, more to say for Vivaldi than the above quotations convey. The great Germans regarded him as a " topping man " among writers of violin concertos, and they made a remarkable study of his works—not the light and flashy ones, but the solid pieces of original and safe form. They saw in the concertos the promise of an architecture that would admit expansion, a rich development, and the utterance therein of their own energetic thoughts and warm emotions.

And so Bach took a batch of these concertos, to arrange and amplify them for performance on other instruments, in that manner he had of getting into the central mind of the art of his time. Sixteen he adapted for the solo clavier. No. 13 of the sixteen—a clear and vigorous movement in C major—he further adapted for the organ, on which instrument it appears as a very jolly solo piece, for the organist at least. A seventeenth work he arranged for four claviers with string quartet ; this was once thought to be an original work of Bach's, and in the early days of the Bach revival in the nineteenth century enthusiasts saw in it the wonder of the great German's art— which, of course, is not in the music. Three other concertos, making twenty in all, he arranged

MAKERS OF MUSIC

for organ solo. Here is the opening of the first of the organ arrangements : it is to be read vivaciously, but with vigour.

VIVALDI AND VERACINI

It was out of such study as that given to the Vivaldi concertos that Bach arrived at his *Italian Concerto* for the clavier, which—if the slow movement is played correctly—is to-day a most pleasant piece for the pianola.

II

This violinist gave a new warmth and brilliance to playing. He attracted many pupils from France, by whom he influenced the art in that country. Several of Corelli's pupils came to him when they had finished their work with the older teacher. Among these last was Giovanni Battista Somis (1678-1763), who thus combined the two schools of Corelli and Vivaldi, and whose pupil Pugnani, by studying under Tartini, combined (as I have already said) the manner of Corelli and that of Tartini, eventually sending this unity and blending into his own great pupil Viotti.

We know little of Somis personally, or of his music. He was a native of Piedmont and lived most of his life at Turin.

Vivaldi lived quietly in Italy. Other players settled in foreign countries, as Geminiani and Castrucci, who passed forty or fifty years in England. A few led very wandering lives, of whom the most notable was Francesco Maria Veracini, born the same year as Bach, 1685, and died the same year, 1750.

43

MAKERS OF MUSIC

III

Veracini was one of the impassioned players. His tone was unusually clear, and so full as to dominate the largest band and go into every part of the largest hall or church. He played vivaciously, and with a fanciful buoyancy ; and because his nature was warm and impulsive, inducing him to yield entirely to the spirit of music, folk said he was an eccentric : but Veracini did no more than anticipate the modern idea of violin playing, though he must certainly have appeared extreme to the people accustomed to the prevailing Corellian quietude.

Stories abound of this virtuoso. He was proud, vainglorious and arrogant, and other musicians did not like him. In Italy they called him *capo pazzo,* which means Hot-Head, with an accompanying idea not unlike our *looney.* This man said he was the greatest violinist in the world ; which was probably true, leaving out Tartini, though he need not have said it by any means except his fiddle. He had two Steiner violins, which he named St. Peter and St. Paul, and he coupled himself with the Almighty, saying that as there was one God of creation, so there was one Veracini of violin playing. All this got on the nerves of the Germans in particular, and at Dresden, in 1720, the court musicians played a trick on him that had serious consequences : they arranged matters so that he had to play a difficult concerto at sight, and then they had the piece repeated immediately by a member of the band who (unknown to Veracini and the audience) had carefully prepared it ; in his rage at the appearance of an apparently equal performer, Veracini, it is said, threw himself out of a window, so that for the rest of his life he went lame. Once he had to play at a church festival, and going to the head seat, found it occupied by an old player named Laurenti, who had always sat there on these occasions, and who—having been away for some years in Poland—knew not Veracini. In a huff, Veracini insisted on occupying the lowest seat of all ; from which in due time he played his solo, in such a manner as to make the audience-congregation cry out in approval, while every now and then Veracini turned towards old Laurenti and shouted, " That's the way to play the violin " ; the old man probably showing his disgust, and taking plenty of snuff.

Veracini was a good musician in every way. He wrote operas, one of which was given in London in 1735, with Farinelli, Senesino and Cuzzoni in the cast ; for these were the years when Handel and his enemies were running Italian opera in England.

But he ended badly. When turned sixty years of age, he was shipwrecked, losing the two violins and all his possessions. It was too late for him to recover, and he passed his last few years of life in poverty, in the town of Pisa.

Veracini left no pupils, since—like Paganini—he would not teach.

V. TARTINI

Veracini and Tartini are opposed in every quality and circumstance. The one was a wanderer, the other a home-lover, who for the last thirty years of his life did not even leave the city where he worked. The one made much money, and died poor ; the other refused to earn large amounts of money, and he would never let profitable engagements interfere with his work, yet he left a fair sum behind him. The virtuoso was vain to the point of insanity ; the teacher and scholar was modest to a fault. Veracini bequeathed a name and some stories, Tartini a " school of nations " in his many pupils. The first threw himself out of a window because he thought there was in the room as good a player as himself, the virtuoso, while the second was happy to say that a pupil was greater than himself, the teacher. Tartini was a thinker, an observer, scientist and great composer, Veracini only a great executant and writer of the operas that fade after a season. The younger man still shines like a star, while the elder went like a flashing comet. . . . It is helpful to learn of musicians in antithetical pairs, and so I offer you Tartini and Veracini, as in the larger history of music you are offered Bach and Handel, Schuman and Chopin, and the like—though not, as here, with the violinists in disparagement of one of the pair.

MAKERS OF MUSIC

I

We can believe that Giuseppe Tartini (1692-1770) was a musician of the highest rank but that occupied by the supreme masters of composition. He died the year Beethoven was born, when Haydn was thirty-eight and Mozart fourteen.

The second supreme authority of the violin, and for the last fifty years of his life the acknowledged leader, he joins the old world of music to the new, in several important respects ; but the new world of Haydn, Mozart, and Beethoven was so immediate and complete that it practically overwhelmed all his work apart from the art of playing : his theoretical and scientific writings are forgotten, and we do not use much of his music.

Tartini was not a revolutionary, yet he was an individualist in the modern way, and it was his belief that the musician must express himself in his art.

In the generations before him, music was not powerfully influenced by its composer. The man's personality conditioned his work, of course, and Byrd and Palestrina wrote music that is different, not only because they were English and Italian respectively, but also because they were Byrd and Palestrina. Yet there is not the difference between them that there is between Haydn and Mozart, or Chopin and Schumann, and in their time all true musicians could write

48

the same kind of music, so that without close study and the rarest sensitiveness the pieces could not be told apart.

Tartini was one of the first composers to realize that music may, and should, contain the personality of its maker. He took the old forms of sonata and concerto, and charged them with a new character, which was peculiar to himself. Generally such music as his lives ; but in his case it was submerged under something of still greater personality that ensued immediately, namely the music of the Mozart, Haydn and Beethoven school.

II

His father, a wealthy man living in Pirano, wanted Giuseppe to study theology, with a view to entering the Church. Both father and son were religious ; but the son was too vivacious, too active mentally and physically, and too warmly interested in things, to tolerate the idea of living the professional life of the Church ; though this would have interfered little with the musical life he desired almost from the first. Giuseppe was very strong ; as a swordsman he was famous, and altogether he wanted an active intellectual life. Moreover, he had a warm and general love of art.

There were discussions that left the father not very well disposed to his son, and the two parties compromised, Giuseppe entering the university of Padua as a student of law. This was in 1709, when he was seventeen.

Here he worked well. But it was not long before music, and especially the violin, called too strongly to be resisted ; and the boy came to the conclusion that he must live for music. Casting about for means of existence, since music would bring in nothing for some years, he actually settled on the idea of establishing a school for fencing, which would take up only a part of his time and bring in enough money for his support. Help from home could not be relied on, if once he forsook his law studies.

But these plans and projects were demolished by the simple act of falling in love. Giuseppe's sweetheart was the niece of an eminent church-man ; the love was laughed at, and marriage ridiculed and forbidden. Naturally, Giuseppe and the girl married secretly. But this put Giuseppe in serious danger. For the marriage being discovered, a warrant was issued for his arrest.

Imprisonment at the command of the Church was a terrible thing in those days, and the young husband had to flee, leaving his wife behind him in Padua. Elizabetta Premazone would be lonely and sad ; but I suggest you do not pity her more than a little, because she was a masterly kind of person, who made the people round her miser-able enough if she could not have her own way,

and whose tongue was the tongue of a virtuoso.

Giuseppe got to Rome in the disguise of a
monk. Rome was not safe, and so he had to
wander for some months about the country,
until he reached a monastery at Assisi. Here the
head was a relation of his. Secret shelter was
given him ; and for two years Giuseppe lay
hidden, passing for a lay member of the
community.

He filled his time with study of violin playing,
scientific investigation in the nature of musical
sounds, performance in the services, and composition. One of the works written at this time
was that sonata called *Il trillo del diavolo*, of
which the story is too well-known to call for
re-telling. At this time also he discovered those
features of acoustics which were called " Tartini's
tones " until Helmholtz discovered their principles a hundred and fifty years later, since when
they have been called Differential Tones. Tartini experimented with the strings and with the
bow, making the strings thicker and the bow
lighter.

The performances of the mysterious stranger
drew large congregations, and his company was
profitable. He used to play behind a curtain.
One day this blew aside, or was inadvertently
drawn back by one of the officiating priests, and
the player was revealed. There was a man from
Padua in the church, who recognized Tartini,

and sent the news on to Padua that the missing man was at Assisi.

III

Trouble was expected : but two years had passed, and Tartini had proved himself in music. Therefore the father and the cardinal-uncle pardoned the disobedient couple, and they lived openly in Padua.

Tartini also lived openly in the profession of music, probably with a return of his father's allowance. The first episode of his new life with which I am acquainted relates to Veracini. The virtuoso was to give a great display of his skill in Venice, in the year 1716 ; and it was arranged that Tartini, already famous in Northern Italy, should compete with him. But shortly before the date of the contest Tartini heard Veracini play at Cremona. To his surprise, he saw at once that he had much to learn. He knew he was a strong player, aided by his finely tempered muscles (a fine violinist has muscles in his arms, legs and loins that an athlete would almost envy) ; but he perceived that Veracini had discovered and solved problems of which he himself had not suspected even the existence. So he withdrew from the contest, retired from Padua, and entered on a further course of study.

He was now twenty-four. We understand that this great player had no real instructor at

TARTINI

any time. His first master, a modestly gifted musician named Giulio di Terni, had soon become his pupil ; and altogether it seems that Tartini evolved his fine art from within, by thought, observation, experience and continuous practice, and by the aid of Corelli's compositions. He had worked hard before this experience of Veracini, and he worked hard after it ; yet he used to say late in life that he had really done very little work until he was turned thirty.

Years passed, until in 1721 he was honoured with an important office, which was the leadership of the musicians in the Capella del Santo in Padua. In 1723 he went for two years to Prague ; but Bohemia and the Bohemians made him miserable, first by reason of the natures of the people and the conditions they supported, but chiefly because of the intense love this man had of home, and his deep longing for a life of perfect quietude and stability. No German, not even Bach, loved his home and private work-room more than Giuseppe Tartini.

It was in 1728 that he established his school in Padua. More than forty years of life lay before him. From about the age of fifty, on to his death at nearly eighty, he did not once leave Padua. . . .

This is the full story of his outward life. Only a wise and genial philosopher could tell the story of his inner life. He resisted all proffered engagements to go into Germany, France and

53

England. Large sums were offered, even three thousand pounds for a few concerts ; but he merely said, " We are not rich, but there is sufficient." Occasionally a rumour spread that he was going to Paris or London, and there was great excitement ; but nothing came of the rumour, because he firmly intended never to travel. Perhaps Elizabetta had something to do with this, for she was a nervous woman, whose self-will strengthened itself with age. . . . They had no children ; home life might have been more placid otherwise : but Tartini loved his wife ; his loyalty was perfect, and his work protected him against the ordinary complaining of every day.

IV

There is, in the history of music, nothing more rare, delightful and encouraging than the record of Tartini's regard for his pupils. Some teachers grow jealous of gifted pupils ; they fear to have them around, and turn them out, even from the academies and schools of which they are the head —picking a quarrel, or making life miserable for the student : such musicians are generally failures, proved so before they get to the end of their lives.

Tartini longed to have pupils as advanced as himself, and he was proud to have some excuse for saying that a pupil was *more* advanced—

for he liked other people to know of the skill of
the young violinists under him. If a student was
gifted, hard-working and affectionate, Tartini
loved him ; and the pupil loved the teacher in
return.

Two of his many hundreds of pupils are
conspicuous in this respect—Nardini and Bini.
But all who knew him seem to have loved him,
so warm was their regard for his private character
and public conduct.

Nardini came from Leghorn to be with him
in the last days of his life and to help to soothe
him in dying (his death was painful, the cause
being cancer in the foot and a kind of paralysis)
and he remained for the funeral, to honour his
removal to the grave.

A book on Tartini was published the year of
his death : a long poem in his praise had been
written as far back as the year 1753, by the
Abbate Vincenzo Rota, of Padua ; and after his
death he was much eulogized.

It was endless generosity, private and artistic,
that maintained this surrounding atmosphere of
love and respect. Tartini, unlike Corelli, left
his money to his poor relations. More than
this, when he knew that he must die, he dis-
tributed it immediately, that they should have at
once the convenience of the legacy, and that he
might see their ease and happiness. Thus he
filled the last year or so of his life with a fresh,
final activity of gratitude ; and he saw true regret

55

at his passing, none waiting to benefit by his actual death.

Pasqualino Bini, Nardini, Domenico Ferrari, Johann Gottlieb Graun, the famous Pugnani, André Noel Pagin and Madelena Lombardini (Madame Sirmen, to whom he addressed a letter of instruction in playing), are among his more eminent pupils.

v

Tartini had the strongest admiration for Corelli's music. He had himself carried further the art of playing, but knew his advance derived from Corelli, to whom he gave all the credit. And so he made his pupils form themselves on the music of the earlier man—chiefly on the solo pieces, Op. 5, before he let them take the music of others, especially his own. This was, perhaps, one main cause of the universal popularity of Corelli's music up to the beginning of the nineteenth century.

You may be sure a man is among the helpful artists of the world, if he respects the immediate past, while himself a progressive.

His own playing was affected by the fact that. unlike Veracini, he had no desire to shine before a varied and miscellaneous public. Here was no false humility, or any indolence. It was not. indeed, humility of any kind, but a serene contentment with the deep and quiet things of the world, with thought, intellectual achievement, and the permanencies of art—a contentment German rather than Italian.

In the beginning his style was brilliant ; but all his life he was affected by the *recitativo parlante* music of singers, whether it was operatic or (like that of the gondoliers) traditional, and he had a continuous love of singing-tone and melody; and so it happened that quite late in life, when he was more than fifty, he changed his style and gave up the bravura for the graceful and expressive. He was truly the progressive artist, who watches the development of his own nature and adapts his art to it. Bini heard of this change ; and though safely established in Rome, he dropped his work and went back to Padua, to study another year with his loved master.

The people now said of Tartini, " He sings, not plays, on the violin," and an English traveller named Wiseman, wrote, " His adagio was the most *cantabile* and divine of all players I ever remembered."

VI

This change, or rather final manifestation of growth, took place in 1744. The music written after 1744 is that of the " second manner." His bowing had become more elastic, until it was as the throat of the singer, which is the most flexibly expressive of all instruments. The first

57

hundred years of the *bel canto* had led to that long
note of Farinelli's,* with its ravishing *crescendo*
and *diminuendo* ; and the first phase of violin
playing had led thus to the instrumental equiva-
lent of the *bel canto* : the same was the case with
piano playing in the first half of the nineteenth
century, when pianists developed the singing-
tone, and with pianola playing early in the
twentieth, when we learned how to play a melodic
sostenuto, converting the machine into an instrument of music.

But Tartini still held the violin on the right
side of the string-holder, a position that restricts
the finger-work of the left hand.

His music retains the classical dignity of the
Corellian school, but with a new individual
feeling and the grace of a different personality.
In order to express and retain an exact poetic
mood, it was his custom to compose to a phrase
from a poet, generally Petrarch. This phrase he
would write in cypher at the head of his manuscript, and when playing the piece he would
keep it constantly in mind. No doubt he explained the matter to his advanced pupils. One
of the phrases thus used was, " Turn laughter
to tears, O my soul ! "

And so Tartini was truly poetical. There
was pathos in Corelli, but in Tartini a dreamy,
brooding melancholy, of which Browning might
have written, had he not been deflected by the

* See page 252

unknown " toccata " of Galuppi. As always in art, this brooding melancholy was companioned by a great manly vigour ; and the music called for a broad and varied intellectuality in performance. But the greater power and pathos of the early eighteenth century are in the music of Bach and (in smaller degree) Handel.

Tartini published several books, pamphlets, and essays on music, its theory, science and executive principles. Twenty or thirty other literary works remain in manuscript. One lengthy work was lost, owing to the death of the man to whom he had entrusted it for posthumous publication. He was always interested in acoustics, and taught his pupils to play double notes by aid of that Differential Tone which proves just intonation.

VI. FROM TARTINI
TO VIOTTI

PIETRO NARDINI (1722-1793) who of all
Tartini's affectionate pupils seems to have been
most attached to his master, was born in a Tuscan
village named Fibiana ; but he counts for a
native of Leghorn, for the reason that his people
moved there while he was a baby.

He finished his work with Tartini when
twenty-four years old, which means that he knew
Tartini only when the latter was middle-aged
and that his love for him was as a son's for his
father. Thirty years stood between the two.

Nardini held an important post at Leghorn,
and then went for fifteen years into the service
of the Duke of Wurtemburg, playing at the court
in Stuttgart. The German musicians, and in
particular Mozart's father, thought very highly
of him. The fifteen years expired, Nardini came
back to Leghorn, from which place he went to
be with Tartini during the last days of his old
master's life, as told above : he was now forty-
eight years old, and his love and high regard
were evidently of a perfect sincerity. From 1770
to the year of his own death Nardini was solo
violinist and music director to the Duke of
Tuscany.

Having studied under Tartini after the old
master had perfected his expressive style, Nardini

was the chief representative of that style ; he was not a *brilliant* performer, and Leopold Mozart's criticism of his art is exactly the same as that of all other writers who have mentioned him : " The beauty, purity, and equality of his tone, and the tastefulness of his *cantabile* playing, cannot be surpassed, but he does not execute great difficulties."

His manner was grateful to the Germans, who have always preferred the expressive to the bravura in violin playing. Christian Friedrich Schubart, the poet and musician, who is persistently sentimental, said that Nardini's playing brought tears into the eyes of the stony-hearted courtiers, and that his own tears ran down the violin as he played : if true, this argues a good supply from the violinist's eyes.

Some of his compositions (*e.g.*, a Sonata in D major, and a Larghetto in D major) were played at London concerts forty or fifty years ago.

One of Nardini's pupils was Thomas Linley, the friend of Mozart. These two were born the same year (1756). They met at Florence, and the friendship that sprang up between them had that love which sometimes comes between boys of a warm nature. In 1778, when twenty-two years old, Linley was drowned at Grimsthorpe, in Lincolnshire, through the upsetting of a boat.

MAKERS OF MUSIC

Domenico Ferrari (died 1780), mentioned above as one of Tartini's greater pupils, did not assume his master's expressive style, but developed the bewildering manner of the virtuoso. His harmonics were immaculate, and he played running octaves as though they were single notes.

Ferrari was a member of the court band at Stuttgart at the same time as Nardini. It is said that he was murdered in Paris.

Indirectly, and very curiously at second-hand, a connection exists between Ferrari and Karl Ditters von Dittersdorf (1739-1799). This man was a Viennese, whose teacher of the violin was a musician named Trani. Trani, a close friend of the Italian (whom the people of Vienna adored), was able to play exactly in the Ferrari manner, and equally able to convey that manner to such a gifted pupil as Dittersdorf. The latter in his youth was such a perfect copy of Ferrari—whom he had never even heard play—that in Vienna he was called Ferrari's little ape. Dittersdorf was an important composer of his time ; his chamber music is delightful hearing even to-day, particularly when given by a body of players like the Catterall String Quartet. On his death-bed he dictated a long autobiography, which is one of the brightest books written about music : it was translated into English by A. D. Coleridge, and published in 1896. This book, more than any other, shows us the character of the musical tastes in Austria and Germany in the generation before Beethoven.

III

Gaetano Pugnani (1731-1798), who was pupil of Tartini and of Somis (and therefore in the direct line with Corelli), need not be carried in the student's mind except as the teacher of Viotti. Viotti was one of the great violinists of Paris at the end of the eighteenth century ; his pupils conveyed the Italian tradition to the musicians who studied under them ; and so this Pugnani is a vital link in the story of violin playing.

Pugnani was a pleasant man, curiously ugly, with a terrific nose and an ungainly body.

VII. VIOTTI & THE FRENCH

THERE were many violinists in France in the time of Tartini, and also in the earlier time of Corelli. A few of these were good performers, who in a general history of violin playing would afford interesting material for writing and reading.

But the French were not the equal of the Italians until their ideas were strengthened, and their practice conditioned, by the Tartini school. Then they rapidly overtook and surpassed the Italians, so that for fifty years the great violinists of the world came from Paris.

The art then shifted into Germany, until several of the supreme violinists of the nineteenth century arose in that part of Europe, and in Bohemia, Poland, and Russia.

I

Jean Maria Leclair (1697-1764) is the first French player to be mentioned here. He was five years younger than Tartini.

Originally a dancer and ballet-master, he played the violin only for amusement and for the convenience of his profession : dancing-masters generally carried a small instrument with them, called a kit, on which they played their accompaniments, even while dancing themselves.

Leclair met Somis in Italy, where he had gone in connection with a ballet, and Somis advised him to study the violin seriously, offering him instruction. The Frenchman was not long in developing a good technique ; he was vivacious and graceful, a master of that pathos which the Italians cultivated, and light and swift in his bowing ; he was also properly French, having a liking for that ballet-like pomposity which had always been characteristic of the violin-music of his nation : but when he got back to Paris, he found that the violinists there did not approve of the dancer turned fiddler. All kinds of obstacles were put in his way. It was hard for him to play in public, or even in the theatre orchestras ; and before he reached the age of forty he gave up striving to make a public position, but withdrew into private life, where he filled his time with composition and teaching. In the long run, this was better for the general art of the violin, for he was a good teacher and a perfect musician.

We do not know the cause of the crime ; but Leclair was murdered just outside his house one evening, when sixty-seven years old.

Fifty years separate Leclair and Viotti. Leclair belongs to French violin art before it found itself, Viotti to the same when it was becoming the most highly individual in history. His life was curiously diversified, and it ended unhappily, though the cause was chiefly his own lack of steadfastness.

MAKERS OF MUSIC

II

Giovanni Battista Viotti (1753-1824) was a Piedmontese, the son of a blacksmith. His father was a fair amateur musician, a performer on the horn and a student of theory.

Giovanni learned to play a little on the violin before he was eight. Three years later he had some lessons from a wandering lute-player. These were probably good, for the wanderer was a gifted musician who, shortly after, had a valuable official post given him.

When thirteen, Giovanni became acquainted with the flute-player Jean Pavia. Pavia introduced the boy to a bishop, and the bishop introduced him to a nobleman who wanted someone to study side by side with his son. At first the nobleman thought Giovanni too young for this post, because his son was eighteen, and he was for sending him back home. But a musician of the household had heard Giovanni play a difficult piece of music at sight ; he informed the nobleman of this achievement, and after the boy had been further tested with a work of Ferrari's, the nobleman adopted him musically. He sent him to Pugnani, and expended on his education the sum of seven hundred and fifty pounds.

After three or four years' work under this pupil of Tartini and Somis, Viotti went out on a long concert tour. The tour lasted two years, Pugnani travelling with Viotti for the first few months.

66

VIOTTI AND THE FRENCH

They were a well-contrasted pair, the master ugly and clumsy, the pupil graceful, charmingly dignified, and beautiful of face.

Concerts were given in Switzerland, Dresden, Berlin (where Viotti played with the King of Prussia, Mara's despotic employer), Poland, Russia, and finally Paris.

Viotti reached Paris the same year as Mara got there.* He intended to remain a few weeks, and stayed ten years.

One of his first appearances was at a benefit concert for Mara. It was the custom then for musicians to give and receive help in this way, and if *A* sang or played for *B*, in return *B* would play or sing for *A*, when the time came round for his benefit. Mara promised to sing for Viotti ; but his success at her benefit had been so great as to arouse her jealousy, and on the night of his concert she did not turn up.

The Mara-Todi war raged next year, and I have no doubt Viotti was properly disgusted.

He was now twenty years old. Within a year of coming to Paris he became very famous in the city. He played a good deal, yet his fee did not reach four pounds, while Mara could command a hundred, and fifty years later Paganini could make a thousand at a single concert.

Now, as always, he played in the classical manner of Corelli and Tartini, but with the modern warmth and larger grandeur, and with

* See page 276

a full measure of his own personality. Ease and grace, superimposed on nobility, were the essential qualities of his art ; and all his work, as composer and as player, owned a fine dignity. There was, in the expression of his face, a beautiful light—the light of a man of amiable mind. He was vivacious, open, proud in the right way, and always pleasant. Musicians looked on his concertos and other large works as the equal of Mozart's compositions of the same kind : several of these are still in use. (In all, he wrote more than two hundred works, among them examples of the largest forms in which the violin and the orchestra enter.)

But a life of public success did not content him—either this, or he was fundamentally unsettled. For the public, with their fickle and irresponsible likes and dislikes, he had no respect. The aristocracy he scorned for their superficiality. And so, when only twenty-one years old, he dropped his public work and withdrew into the private life of a teacher. Tartini had refused to be the pet of the public. Liszt, at the age of thirty-seven, ceased to play the piano as a concert-virtuoso. It seems that the true musician is unable to bear the strain and secret degradation of a popular fame.

Viotti, however, was happy to play to any sincere music-lovers ; and he attached himself officially to the Queen, Marie Antoinette. He and Cherubini, then twenty-six or twenty-seven, lived together for a while. They gave private concerts in their house, and Viotti introduced Cherubini to the Queen and other persons of influence.

This went on for four years, when Viotti joined with others in re-establishing Italian opera in Paris, Italian opera having been dormant there for ten years. He put all his money into the venture, all his thought and energy, and all his time. Being a fine artist, he determined that the revival should be a matter of fine art, whatever the cost and labour. His fellow-directors sent him into Italy to gather together and engage the finest company of singers available ; and he left no means inactive to build up in the city a beautiful opera.

He and his companions succeeded ; but the Revolution came. They struggled on until 1792 ; and then, his money lost and his grand efforts wasted, Viotti had to leave Paris, ten years after he entered it.

III

He came to London, and resumed his life of a public performer. Salomon, the German violinist who had been settled in London since 1781, and at whose concerts Haydn appeared with his famous " Salomon " symphonies, engaged him, and he played in that 1794 series of concerts, whereat Haydn made his second appearance in this country.

Viotti was doing well, teaching actively, and happy in some friends he had made, of which the principal were Mr. and Mrs. Chinnery, when suddenly, in 1798, he was banished the country, the government suspecting—falsely—that he was an agent of the French revolutionary government.

This was a severe blow, and the second fatal shock to his fortunes. He settled in a small place near Hamburg, and for three years wrote music and gave lessons. Pupils came to him from a distance, among them Pixis, whose name enters into several branches of musical history. In 1801 he was allowed to return to London.

But now Viotti seemed tired of a musical life, or else he found it hard for a foreigner, once suspected of republican sympathies, to recover standing with the British public. He therefore went into business, borrowing money from the Chinnerys and setting up as a wine-merchant. Early in his business life he went over to Paris for some months, where he was warmly welcomed by Baillot and other musicians ; but from 1803 to 1813 he was fairly out of touch with music.

Viotti was a poor business man. By 1813, which was the sixtieth year of his age, he was compelled to take to music again ; and by 1818 he was ruined, with his debts still owing. Those debts were a painful trouble, for he was a proud and honourable man.

The Royal Philharmonic Society was established in 1813, Viotti and Salomon being among the founders.

Ruined in business, no longer with the energy even of middle age (for he was sixty-six), and unhappy in owing money to friends, Viotti went over to Paris, to try a second venture in opera. This started well, and promised well ; but misfortune attended, as it had attended nearly thirty years ago upon his first operatic enterprise : a year from the opening of the theatre, the Duc de Berry, a relative of the King, was assassinated in the building ; the deed cast a gloom over the place, and though they moved to another, the opera was doomed.

Viotti, nearly seventy years old, had not even the furniture needed to make a living-room habitable. He came back to London, went to his faithful friends, Mr. and Mrs. Chinnery, and lived with them (occasionally taking short journeys as a means of distraction) until he died. What he left behind him was a gold watch, two good violins, two gold snuff-boxes, and his clothes— and those old debts, which on his death-bed seem almost to have broken his proud and gentlemanly nature.

This man is called by historians and critics *the father of modern violin-playing, and one of the most important composers for this instrument.* He wrote the following works :

29 violin concertos
2 concertante for two violins

MAKERS OF MUSIC

21 string quartets
21 trios for two violins and cello
51 violin duets
18 violin sonatas
3 divertissements
9 piano sonatas
10 piano concertos

and other miscellaneous pieces, all of which left him poor.

VIII. THE PARIS SCHOOL

A BRILLIANT school of violinists lived and worked
in Paris after Viotti left in 1792. From the
members of this school stretch many lines of
master and pupil, which in our own time run to
such players as Tor Aulin, Ysaye, Brodsky,
Kreisler, Mischa Elman, Zimbalist, von Vecsey,
Willy Burmester, Jacques Thibaud, and César
Thompson.

To attempt to tell the story of the original
members of the school and of their influence
would defeat my present object, which is to
indicate the main features of the rise and extension
of violin playing and to make clear the character
of a few representative performers. The full
story would be as complex as the first chapter of
the Gospel of St. Matthew or the chronological
table of the descendants of King Charles the
Second. Indeed, it would be more complex than
these, for it would have to embrace an account
of the development of modern music at the hands
of violinists, and to include an account of the
many young prodigies of the violin who appeared
after the year 1880.

I may therefore do no more than mention a
few of the Parisian violinists who lived at the
dawn of the nineteenth century, so as to clear
the way for the stories of two very remarkable
individualists of this art—Paganini and Ole
Bull.

73

MAKERS OF MUSIC

I

Pierre Baillot (1771-1842) strikes more power-fully on the mind than any other of the school after Viotti. Before we know much about him, he appears as something admirable—as a man sensible, warm-hearted, earnest, generous, physically and mentally strong, and highly gifted ; also as a man blessed with an enthusiasm that is not to be scorned because it often ran away with him. . . . Not all the Parisian musicians were admirable persons in the first quarter of the century : the young Mendelssohn, in the year 1825, "met Hummel, Moscheles, Kalkbren-ner, Pixis, Rode, Baillot, Kreutzer, Cherubini, Rossini, Paër, Meyerbeer, Plantade, Lafont, and many others, often in the same *salon* and the same opera-box, but of many of whom the mean-ness, jealousy, and enviousness made a repulsive impression." Baillot was not one of these repul-sive individuals.

He did not take lessons from Viotti, yet we can call him a pupil of Viotti even more directly than we can call Dittersdorf a pupil of Ferrari. His father, a schoolmaster, put him to learn the violin first under an Italian and secondly under a Frenchman, each of whom gave the boy methodi-cal training. When Pierre was twelve, his father died ; but a highly-placed government official took him in hand and sent him to Italy to study under a pupil of Nardini, that loving disciple of Tartini's who was with his master when he died.

This Nardini pupil was named Pollani, and from him Baillot received the traditions of the Italian classical school.

He did not become a professional musician for a considerable time. For five years after his return from Italy, he lived in the south of France with his benefactor, helping him as private secretary.

At the age of twenty, Baillot felt he must live in music, and so made his way to Paris. Here he played to Viotti, who thought well of his abilities and helped him to a good post. Baillot had heard Viotti in one of his concertos when a boy of ten, and had always carried Viotti in mind as the model of what he himself hoped to be in the future.

Even now, however, he could not remain with music ; the army claimed him for two years, and for some time further he had to work in a government department. It was not until 1795 that he entered finally on a musical life. In that year, his gifts being widely known and admitted, he with several other violinists became professors at the newly established Conservatoire.

It is from these professors that the great stream of performers flowed.

Baillot was not a good theoretical musician at this time, so he set to work, working very hard at all branches and generally perfecting himself. Ten years later he went for three years to Russia, making money and winning fame. Further on in life he toured in Italy, Switzerland, the Netherlands and England ; but for the most part he lived in France, teaching, and developing those methods of instruction and performance which are still in use. Baillot filled several official posts, under Napoleon and the King ; and he was much drawn to chamber music.

The classical qualities of violin playing—a clear and full tone, just intonation, entire neatness, and a lofty idea for the music rather than for the execution, were combined in Baillot with the French qualities of violin playing—animation, fine mental vigour, a definiteness of expression as concrete almost as the movement of dancers or the actions of singers, and that soaring ecstasy and glowing fervour which the French call *élan*.

Accounts of his playing abound in books and essays. The following is from a letter written home from Paris by Mendelssohn, on April 10th, 1825. It lets us see how the typical French manner of Baillot, now fifty-four years old, struck a young German musician—Mendelssohn being sixteen :

THE PARIS SCHOOL

You say I should try to convert the people here, and teach Onslow and Reicha to love Beethoven and Sebastian Bach. That is just what I am endeavouring to do. But remember, my dear child, that these people do not know a single note of *Fidelio*, and believe Bach to be a mere old-fashioned wig stuffed with learning. . . .

Rode persists in his refusal to touch a violin. But the other day I played my quartet in B minor at Mme. Kiené's, with Baillot, Mial, and Norblin. Baillot was rather confused at the beginning, and played even carelessly, but at one passage in the first part of the first movement he caught fire, and played the rest of the movement and the whole adagio very well and with much vigour. Then came the scherzo ; and he must have liked the beginning, for now he began to play and hurry in earnest, the others after him, and I in vain trying to stop them. But who can stop three runaway Frenchmen ? And so they took me with them, madder and madder, and faster and louder. Baillot especially, at a place near the end, where the theme of the trio is taken up against the time, played fearfully loud ; and as it had happened to him to make a mistake several times before, he got into a perfect rage with himself. When he had finished, he said nothing but, " Encore une fois ce morceau." Now everything went on smoothly, but wilder

even than before. In the place quite near the
end, where the theme in B minor comes in
once more fortissimo, Baillot produced a
hurricane in the strings that put me in fright
of my own quartet. And as soon as it was
finished, he came up to me, again without
saying a word, and embraced me twice as if he
wanted to crush me. Rode was also very much
pleased, and a long while afterwards said
again, " Bravo, mein schatz ! " *in German.*

III

Among Baillot's pupils was François Antoine
Habeneck (1781-1849), the violinist and conductor of whom we read many interesting things
in the story of the early life of Berlioz. Habeneck
had for pupil Delphin Alard (1815-1888), a
brilliant virtuoso of the Paganini and Ole Bull
type : this Alard was the master of Sarasate.

André Robberechts (1797-1860), a Belgian,
was one of Baillot's pupils who also had lessons
from Viotti. His chief pupil was De Bériot,
husband of Malibran : from De Bériot we reach
Vieuxtemps, and from the latter Ysaye.

The Rode mentioned in Mendelssohn's letter
was Jacques Pierre Joseph Rode (1774-1830),
a pupil of Viotti. One of Rode's pupils was
the famous Bohemian teacher Joseph Böhm
or Boehm (1798-1876), who has more great
violinists in the record of his teaching than any

other master : Ernst, Singer, Hellmesberger, L. Strauss, Rappoldi, Dont, Jacob Grün, Reményi, and Joachim.

Dont taught Auer, and Auer taught Mischa Elman and Zimbalist.

Georg Hellmesberger taught his son Josef, who in turn taught Brodsky and Kreisler.

Joachim pupils are great in number, and I need only mention Hubay, the master of von Vecsey.

All these pupils and grandpupils of Böhm studied in Vienna, or wherever in Germany the violinists had settled themselves.

IV

Rode, who " persisted in his refusal to touch a violin " again, was a man who failed after a brilliant beginning. He travelled about a good deal, and was so fine a player that Spohr, who heard him in 1803, when Spohr was nineteen, strove for a long while to base his own style on Rode's. But Rode's playing began to deteriorate as early as 1808. Spohr heard him again in 1811, and was disappointed. Beethoven, who in that year finished for Rode the great sonata in G, Op. 96, was not satisfied with his performance of the work. And so in 1814 Rode retired. Once, a few years later, he made an appearance in public, but the result was disastrous.

Rode, through Böhm, takes us from the Paris

school into .the Austrian-German of the nine-
teenth century. Another member of the Paris
school, Rudolph Kreutzer, who with Rode and
Baillot compiled the Violin Method used at the
Conservatoire, links us retroactively with the
German school of the eighteenth century.

Kreutzer was a German, but born in France,
where his teachers were his father, a performer
in the King's band, and Anton Stamitz.

v

The Stamitzes were a family of Bohemian
musicians who settled in Mannheim in 1745.
The father, Johann Wenzl Karl (1717-1761),
was a self-taught musician, who wrote nearly
fifty symphonies in the manner that Haydn was
immediately to develop, leading to Mozart and
Beethoven. He and his brother were chief
violinist and chief cellist respectively in the
Electoral band. It was in Mannheim that modern
orchestral playing first appeared, and for this the
Stamitzes are famous in history. One of the
sons, Carl, who wrote about seventy of these
symphonies, remained in Germany ; the other,
Anton, went to Paris.

The Stamitzes were the founders of what is
called the Mannheim school of violin playing,
which in varying measure claims such later men
as Spohr, Cramer, Kalliwoda, Pixis, and Sevcik,
the teacher of Kubelik, and a thousand others.

THE PARIS SCHOOL

The actual Mannheim style was looked on as antiquated even in the time of Mozart, and if we could hear one of the Stamitzes play to-day, we should be dissatisfied with the coldness of the style.

The truly great German violin playing is a blending of the Parisian manner, with its Italian tradition and French *élan*, and of the poetic warmth of the Germans and the rich feeling of the Austrians and Bohemians.

Rudolph Kreutzer (1766-1831) became famous in Paris at the age of sixteen. He made a great tour in 1796, becoming acquainted with Beethoven, who gave him the dedication of that sonata which we call the "Kreutzer." His pupil, Lambert Joseph Massart, a Belgian, taught Henri Wieniawski.

VI

During the period of Baillot, Kreutzer, Rode, and the other Parisians I have spoken of, lived a Frenchman who was the most candid charlatan-virtuoso named in history. This was Alexandre Jean Boucher (1778-1861), self-taught, and self-managed. He was a child prodigy, playing at the French court when six, and at important concerts in Paris when eight. At the age of nine he was appointed solo violinist to the King of Spain, holding this office for nearly twenty years—from 1787 to 1806. He then lived in Paris until 1820 ; after which, at the age of forty-two, he began to travel abroad.

Boucher was second only to Paganini, his contemporary, in all the elements of virtuosity. His swift playing, his double stopping and staccato, were miraculous ; and he was a fair musician.

But he aped the peculiar, and found it profitable ; as did his wife, who played duets with herself on the piano and the harp, one hand on each instrument. At the climax of a furious passage Boucher would snap the bridge of his fiddle out of place, and he pulled faces and twisted his legs and body in a manner impossible to Pachmann, because a pianist has to sit at his instrument.

Having a close likeness to Napoleon, Boucher dressed, walked, took snuff, and arranged his forelock, like Napoleon. He strolled the streets before a concert, acknowledging salutations as Napoleon used to do ; and he advertised that he was forbidden the sacred soil of France, because his likeness to the fallen and banished (and now deceased) emperor moved the sentiments of the French, making them dangerously aware of their loss.

Boucher was about as modest as the singer Caffarelli, who on his house inscribed the words, " Amphion Thebas, ego domum," for he called himself " The Alexander of the Violin," weeping that there were no more worlds for him to conquer in that art.

One would like some gramophone records of his playing, together with a cinema picture of him on the concert platform and in the streets, with the crowds of people following him.

IX. PAGANINI

I

THERE are unfortunate persons born, who more than any other need wisdom, kindness, and consideration in those who have to look after them in their early days. They are unfortunate, because their nature is defective—weak where it ought to be strong, and strong where it ought to be weak. When these defects are both physical and moral or mental, their misfortune is doubled ; and when the defects are elements in their life as artists, their misfortune is trebled, and the world begins to share in the unhappiness.

Among these unfortunate persons, the violinist Paganini is the supreme member in the art of music. He was defective mentally, morally, physically, and artistically ; and so far as I have observed in reading about him, he never was in association with a man or woman with the power or will to influence him for good. Of course, he was a terribly self-willed individual, and the friend or guardian strong enough to influence him would have been as absolute a rarity as Paganini himself ; yet it is conceivable that Nature might have provided such a helper, had the Fates that presided at his making been other than they were.

His father, Antonio Paganini, is the hatefullest father known in musical history. By his side, Leopold Mozart was a monument of wisdom, and Major von Weber a rich and lovable humorist.

84

PAGANINI

He was a hard, driving, brutal, avaricious man, who brought disgrace on music by having a liking for it. He played the mandoline well, knew something of the fiddle, and had an idea of theory. But his liking was, I imagine, a sentimental fondness, not an intellectual regard or a high spiritualized response : bad characters often have this sentimental fondness for music ; I knew a man who every evening at his pianola cried over the grand harmonies and pathetic melodies of Bach and the impassioned pieces of Beethoven, who was hoggish to his wife, bullying in business, close-fisted, and unable to spend a shilling unless the action resulted in something visible.

Antonio Paganini was such a man, with the further disgrace of cruelty to his son Niccolo.

He was a tradesman of Genoa, in a small way of business. His wife was a gentle and lovable woman. There were four children, two of them boys, of whom Niccolo—born in 1782 (not 1784, as most accounts say)—was the younger.

II

Niccolo was not particularly strong as a child, and when he was ill with a childish complaint at the age of four, his illness affected him so that he lay apparently dead, and it was only by a stroke of luck that he was not buried alive. He showed signs of musical ability about this time,

85

and Antonio at once forced him to an exhausting practice, determined to get money out of the child's gift. If the child did not please him with his work, he locked him up in a room without food, often for a whole day. This of course permanently affected Niccolo's health ; more seriously, it made him nervous, suspicious, and unfriendly.

From about the age of six, Niccolo passed through the hands of various teachers. The first was a second-rate theatre violinist, named Jean Servetto. The next was the leader of music in an important church, named Giacomo Costa. By the time he was eleven, the boy was able to play in public, taking part in concerts at which appeared the famous singer Luigi Marchesi. He played every week in Costa's church, having to prepare a new work for each Sunday : this, Paganini afterwards said, was good for him, making him a quick study and a safe reader at sight.

One of the chief violinists in Italy at this time was Alessandro Rolla, of Parma. In 1795, when thirteen years old, Niccolo wanted to study under him ; and his father consenting, a benefit concert was arranged in Genoa for the purpose of raising money for the journey to Rolla's town. When father and son got to the master's house, he was ill in bed and did not wish to see any visitors. His wife took them into a room, and then went to speak with her husband : while she was away,

PAGANINI

PAGANINI

Antonio saw a piece of manuscript music—Rolla's latest work —on a table, together with a violin ; he told Niccolo to play the music, which the boy did in such manner that Rolla thought some virtuoso must be in the house. He said he could teach the boy nothing, and sent him to the musician and teacher Gasparo Ghiretti. From this clever musician Niccolo received three lessons a week for six months, in violin playing and musical theory. He also, it is believed, had lessons from Rolla, though later in life Paganini said he had not.

In effect, however, Paganini was self-taught, for from the beginning he had ideas so original and individual that no one could help him to define and execute them. He and Rolla had many arguments and disputes, and the boy was what is called a troublesome pupil.

The six months being over, Niccolo withdrew to study by himself. He drafted his famous studies, and worked hard at them. But before long he decided he must thoroughly understand all the various qualities of violin playing, and that he must master the art by observing the successive stages of its growth. He therefore worked systematically through the works of Corelli, Vivaldi, Tartini, Pugnani, and Viotti. It is important to realize the significance of this action on the part of the fourteen-year old youth.

He was still frail, as he was to remain all through his life, and often he was overcome by

87

weariness and illness, which forced him to put work aside for a while. But he laboured on, driven first by his father, and secondly by his great ambition. By 1797 he had written out completely his " Twenty-four Studies " : there were still many of these that he could not play, though working for ten or twelve hours at a stretch at some of them, until he fell down exhausted.

In this year Antonio took him for a tour through Lombardy, which put a fair amount of money into the father's pocket. Niccolo played in Milan, Bologna, Florence, Pisa, Leghorn, and other towns, with much success.

III

Conditions at home got worse rather than better. And so when in the following year Niccolo managed to play at the town of Lucca without the company of his father, he wandered off into other parts of Italy, not returning to Genoa for six years. But Antonio kept his hands on him, and the bulk of his earnings had to be sent home.

These were among the bad years of Paganini's life. He was dissipated, a gambler, and utterly reckless. The slight excuse to be made is, that in the case of such an individual as Paganini, the reaction from the harsh restrictions of home was inevitably of the debased kind. But he had the strength to give up gambling after a year

PAGANINI

or two ; and when his physical and mental powers were exhausted, he was content to live for some time (1801-1804) with a noblewoman in Tuscany, when he did not even play in public.

At the age of twenty-two Paganini went back to Genoa, to work hard at composition, going out regularly into other towns to play at concerts. Not till he was forty-six did he play outside Italy, which unique fact is partly explained by his bad health. But his fame spread widely abroad long before this, and he was one of the most famous musicians in Europe before he visited other countries.

Napoleon was ruler of Italy now. His sister was the Princess of Lucca, afterwards the Grand Duchess of Tuscany ; and from 1805 to 1808 Paganini was her court violinist. It was here that he perfected his art of playing on two strings and on one string ; the latter upset the Princess, because she could not bear the constant harmonics.

His virtuosic career, by which he stands unique in musical history, dates from 1810. This was nearly a quarter of a century since he began to learn under his father ; and so he did not hasten to his high place. In 1812 musicians in Germany began to talk about him, and mystery surrounded his name generally.

Paganini, from now on to 1828, was content to trade on this romance ; he let scandalous stories stand without denial for fifteen years, and not till he went to Vienna in 1828, did he declare he was not the murderer people hinted he was, who had spent years in prison to expiate the murder of his wife. (Those years were the missing years of his young manhood, when he lived with the titled lady in Tuscany.) Even the rumour that he had sold himself to the devil in return for his miraculous skill, and the other rumour that he was a direct child of the Evil One, he allowed to stand, until in Vienna he published a letter from his mother, in which she told him once more how she had prayed that her son might be a great and good musician.

Paganini in 1828 no longer wanted the aid of mystery, gloom, and scandal, and he was upset when he found he could not in a moment destroy the traditions. He was particularly hurt, when, in 1831, the Parisians developed afresh the story of his life in prison.

IV

The years between 1810 and 1828, wherein his fame was so great in Italy, are filled with stories that you may read in the books that deal with Paganini at length.*

In 1817 Antonio Paganini died. In 1815 Niccolo met the dancer Antonia Bianchi, with whom he lived until the end of 1828 ; their son (born 1826) is the child who is often mentioned

*For example, Stephen S. Stratton's *Nicolo Paganini : his Life and Work.* London (" The Strad "), 1907.

PAGANINI

in the story of the last years of Paganini's life, and who was tenderly loved by his father.

In 1823 Paganini nearly died of the intestinal disease which, with other troubles, affected his entire life.

V

It is very curious that until he went to Vienna, in 1828, at the age of forty-six, this renowned man had not been out of Italy, for he was restless, and filled with an inordinate ambition to be before the public.

But he made up for this local activity in the next four years. Vienna went wild over him, and within a few weeks gave his name to boots, soap, sweets, cakes, and so forth, abandoning the city's previous rage for the giraffe that had just been brought into the place and which had previously been used to designate these articles. His head was carved on walking sticks, and the pats of butter were fashioned to his features.

This was the last year of Schubert's life ; his concert took place three days before Paganini's first : Schubert cleared a fortune out of this concert, namely the sum of thirty pounds ; and he paid his six shillings twice to hear the wonderful Paganini.

Spohr met Paganini at this time. They took a meal together, Spohr quiet and refined, Paganini excitable. The German observed in the Italian's musical art a strange mixture of power with triviality, tastelessness, and qualities that were childish.

The years 1829, 1830 and 1831 were filled with concerts in Germany and the adjacent countries, Paris being reached in the March of the last year. Then came the famous visit to London, with the following concerts in English provincial towns, Scotland and Ireland. He cleared about sixteen thousand pounds, above all expenses, out of this visit to the British Isles.

There was a good deal of trouble in London at first, because—having got audiences in Paris at treble the usual prices—Paganini thought it safe to ask double in London. In fact, the concerts originally announced as his opening ones were not given, as only one or two boxes were subscribed for. The papers published many complaints, and Paganini had to give way, dropping the price of the tickets to the normal. His first London concert gave him £700, his second £1,200, his third £900, and so on in varying degrees, the last being comparatively small, because as his audiences, satisfied with what he had to offer, grew smaller, he moved into the concert-room of the London Tavern, in the city —a determined effort to get the last pound possible, which disgusted men like Moscheles.

The people in London irritated Paganini. They flocked round him in the street, getting in front of him and then stopping suddenly in his path to look at him full-face, and sometimes taking him by the arm to see if he were real. This sounds silly, but it happened.

Paganini went back to France and Italy. His health was not good, even in the degree to which he was accustomed, and consumption of the throat began to develop. As far back as 1819, when in Naples, he had seemed ill of consumption, and his landlord had put him and his belongings into the street. In 1823, as already remarked, he had nearly died of an internal complaint. In 1826 he was laid up for months with a disease in one of his legs, and in 1828 he was ill with an abscess in the jaw. His blood generally must have been bad ; and it was too late now for him to recover purity however careful his living.

And so in 1840 he died, the immediate cause being that pulmonary decay of the larynx. He was fifty-eight years old.

VI

Not till 1845 was he properly buried, because he had died without confessing his sins and without receiving absolution : the story is very wretched of what happened to his corpse during those five years—for a long time the coffin lay in an empty house. At last the ecclesiastical authorities were persuaded that the man was not a servant of the devil, and they let his body be laid in consecrated ground.

MAKERS OF MUSIC

Fifty years later, in 1895, his coffin was dug up (apparently out of curiosity), opened, and the contents displayed to the view of persons who wished to see the famous violinist : they say you could distinctly recognize his features, which fact is very interesting and charming.

Niccolo Paganini left £80,000. This money went to his son, except for £1,875 to one of his sisters, and £2,250 to the other, and except for a life-charge of £45 a year to Antonia Bianchi.

Is it worth while telling any stories of Paganini's money-love and avarice ? I think not, because they are without humour, except perhaps that story of his offering a gallery ticket to his servant, if the man would serve him a day for nothing. He demanded such high prices for those of his compositions he cared to publish that the publishers could not take them. He agreed that Moscheles should arrange some of his " Gems " for pianoforte, and then, when Moscheles went ahead with a second and third book, brought a lawsuit, with a claim for damages, against the pianist, declaring that his consent was only for one book. He watched the expenditure of every shilling, and after all lost large sums by bad speculation towards the end of his life. . . . He was, in the matter of money, the true son of Antonio Paganini.

Some of the pictures of Paganini on the concert platform expose him in strained and ridiculous attitudes ; but Mendelssohn's father said he was remarkable for placidity, calmness, and composure, never violent, and perfectly self-possessed ; and other writers, in books written in later years, recollect him as of easy carriage, and dignified as he stood up to play. These reports are worth more than the contemporary accounts of journalists, who naturally had to be attractive rather than truthful, and found it better to say he was grotesque.

VII

His technical ability was as wonderful as anything the world of music has known, though later virtuosos are able to play his music. He astonished chiefly by his playing of a *legato* melody to an accompaniment of *pizzicato* notes and chords. His harmonics were uncanny, first because his ear was immaculately true, and secondly because, while playing, he would suddenly tune a string (by a swift turn of the peg) to a higher note, gaining thereby a fresh set of harmonics, which he used for a moment, returning as swiftly to the original normal tuning. By this and other means, he had that inexhaustible supply of harmonics which, more than anything else, made the people of Catholic countries believe he was sold to Satan. He played harmonics in thirds, sixths, octaves, and shakes. On the G string, his range covered three octaves. His *staccato*, and his repetition of notes, were equal

95   G

to those of the modern pianola, with its eight hundred repetitions in a minute. Above all, he played not only without apparent effort, but with a certainty that struck the people as diabolical, their imaginations not extending to the idea of the angelic.

He played only his own music, and when he occasionally played a Beethoven sonata, musicians of a finer mind than his said the act was desecration. Yet he had a wide knowledge of all violin music, and must for certain have cared for it in his heart. He played on thin strings, " on which alone it was possible to conjure forth those myriads of notes and trills and cadenzas " (says Moscheles), and which would have been useless for other violinists.

But he had none " of Spohr's earnestness, Baillot's power, or even Mayseder's piquancy," and after a few hearings his playing was, for the musician, monotonous, because made up constantly of the same effects. Mendelssohn found that his charm did not persist, and that Paganini's ' eternal mawkishness became at last too much of a good thing."

To-day Paganini would bore us, because our chief joy now is in that classical school which, running from Corelli and Tartini and the German masters of composition, and acquiring the charm and *élan* of the French school in a moderate degree, has permanently filled the world. . . . The opinion of the people who ate the chocolate

PAGANINI

and butter in the likeness of Paganini (if such
people have opinions) does not count here ; but
that of quiet and sane musical amateurs does
count ; and so—to balance the above expressed
opinions of Moscheles and Mendelssohn—I copy
here the most satisfying of all the ideas on
Paganini's art that I have seen recorded. These
next lines are taken from Hermann Klein's
Thirty Years of Musical Life in London (1903),
and the speaker is Klein's old schoolmaster at
Norwich. " Never before or since have I seen
an audience wrought to such a pitch of excitement.
It was partly the influence of the individual
himself, no doubt ; but it was also due to the
strangely wonderful beauty of the tone that he
obtained from his instrument, and the fascination
of a method which completely concealed the
nature of the difficulties he surmounted. As I
listened I seemed to forget that Paganini was a
man. Gradually he assumed the character of a
magician, an executant endowed with positively
supernatural powers."

VIII

Supernatural for his art, and ghost-like for
his appearance, are the words that all writers
use of this man. His face was " sad, pale, wan,
and haggard, with intense pain written in its
deepest lines upon every feature," when he was
seen in England. He came like a ghost on to

the platform, and like a ghost he faded out of company. His body was emaciated, and his hands were bony.

In no way, it seems to me, can this man be admired, except for his hard and close work in youth ; and since that work was not directed to pure art, I cannot see that even this is to be fully admired. His individuality was so terribly distinct that it becomes unnatural to the reflective mind, as much so as the individuality of the madman. Like the glance of a man of despotic power, or of one of those commanders who can will their followers to complete and unquestioning sacrifice, the glance of his eye awed people. This, and his manner, were largely native, but also deliberately cultivated in the manner of the charlatan. Being abnormal, he was removed from common humanity, and he was therefore miserable. I doubt if he ever knew an easy happiness, from the day his twisted nature was ruined by his father, on to the day when he found pleasure in his little son—the handsomest child of the period. He could not know a quiet and easy happiness, because he could not know freedom from suspicion—Paganini never trusted anyone, and though he acted the grateful man to those who did him a kindness, his frequent kisses of thanks struck them as altogether too sweet to be genuine.

His father, a bad man, was never more wicked than when he shaped his son for a perverted

PAGANINI

life ; and though we must dislike Niccolo Paganini, we need despise only Antonio.

How unhappy this man was in the last year of his life is made clear by Charles Hallé's account of his meeting with him in Paris, in 1838, when Hallé was nineteen and Paganini fifty-six. " The striking, awe-inspiring, ghost-like figure of Paganini was to be seen nearly every afternoon in the music-shop of Bernard Latte, Passage de l'Opéra, where he sat for an hour, enveloped in a long cloak, taking notice of nobody, and hardly ever raising his piercing black eyes. He was one of the sights of Paris. . . ." So sat Beethoven, in a tavern, smoking his pipe, with his lonely deafness, but ready to smile on a friend with that smile of recognition which lives in history as almost divine in its perfect humanity. And so sat Schumann in his last years, in a tavern, a glass of beer by his side, whistling softly with his face to the wall and thinking out the music he was composing, his madness upon him, but willing to listen to a friend by the hour, if not worried to answer. But neither Beethoven nor Schumann sat like a ghost.

Yet this poor ghost was lonely, doomed as he knew to die shortly of that terrible wasting disease in his throat. The young Hallé was introduced to him, and invited to his room, where nothing was said, nothing done, except that Paganini would wave his hand towards the piano and Hallé would then play. " Paganini sat there, taciturn, rigid, hardly ever moving a muscle of his face, and I sat spellbound, a shudder running through me whenever his uncanny eyes fell upon me."

The poor man's eyes were uncanny, and he a musician. Here is a sad and fatal contradiction, which makes *us* shudder, as we shudder at the tale of some mysterious power in history. And not only was he a musician, but also a violinist, whose instrument is the most masculine and universally companionable and genial of all, as we learn by the music of Bach, Handel, Haydn, Mozart, Beethoven, Schubert, Schumann, Mendelssohn, and Brahms.

IX

Paganini did little teaching, as is always the case with musicians of his order. One or two players in the first half of the nineteenth century were understood to be his pupils, of whom Ernesto Camillo Sivori (1815-1894) was the only one who could definitely claim him as master. Indeed, Sivori used to announce himself as the sole pupil of Paganini, and the claim passed without much challenge. The story of this man is interesting, and worth the reader's observation at some later date : he had a good time in London in 1843, when the Mario quartet was flourishing here and in Paris.

The principal rival of Paganini among the

PAGANINI

genuine v rtuosos was Karl Joseph Lipinski (1790-1861), a Pole. Lipinski was a more or less self-taught violinist. He and Paganini met in 1817, and were friendly ; but during Paganini's European tour of 1828-1831 they met in severe rivalry in Warsaw, and their friendship was disturbed.—When Lipinski was in Italy, in 1817, he met an ancient pupil of Tartini's, a man ninety or more years of age, to whom he played one of Tartini's compositions ; he could not get the right spirit of the music, and the old man was too feeble to show him what was wanted : but at last the latter called to mind the line from Petrarch which had been the composer's inspiration in the making of the piece ; he quoted this to Lipinski, and then the Polish violinist at once played the music to the old man's satisfaction.

Paganini, having no school of students, did not found a school of violin-playing. But he greatly influenced the Frenchmen of the middle of the nineteenth century, in which period arose that definite kind of playing whish is indicated by the names of Vieuxtemps, Wieniawski, and Sarasate. Opposed to this French manner was the German manner which derived from Paganini's great contemporary, Spohr, and which is indicated by the name of Joachim.

Ludwig Spohr (1784-1859), a native of

Brunswick, has to be written of in the threefold capacity of composer, conductor, and violinist (teacher as well as performer). Here it is necessary only to show how he combines in his art of violin playing the German manner of the middle eighteenth century and the French manner of the end of the eighteenth century, so that you shall clearly understand his relation to Paganini.

Spohr's masters when a child were two Germans, the Rector Riemenschneider, and Maucourt, leader of the ducal band at Brunswick. At the age of eighteen he passed for a year and a half into the hands of Franz Eck (1774-1804).

This Franz Eck, a native of Mannheim, was not connected directly with the Stamitzes (page 80) in Mannheim, but he was naturally affected by them. Viotti and others of the Parisian group influenced his art, and the impression was transmitted by him to his pupil Spohr ; though the latter was by nature inclined to respond to French influence, in particular that of Rode.

Eck was not a particularly good musician, nor a particularly praiseworthy man. He was, indeed, rather a rogue, and so unbalanced in his life that his mind gave way, and he lived his last years in a lunatic asylum.

About the year 1820 Spohr played in Paris ; the musicians there did not respond warmly to him, because they did not care for the romantic energy of his style. The older men, Baillot and

the rest, were established in their manner,
which means that they did not wish to have their
views disturbed ; and the general public were
not particularly interested in what came out of
Germany.

Ten years or so later Paganini entered Paris,
in the manner that I have described above.

X. OLE BULL

With Ole Bull we are in much the same world of music as with Paganini—the world of the virtuoso who lives for the public, not the world of the true artist, who lives for that permanent and continuous art to which we give the name classic ; but otherwise we are in worlds as far apart as a Viking from an unhealthy student of Paris.

Ole Bull was a man whose appearance reminded you of fresh air, clear water, and mountains under a blue sky ; he was almost a giant in strength, tall, fair-haired, and robust enough to wander no less than five times over the United States, the last occasion coinciding with his seventieth birthday : Paganini was a dark-haired, mysteriously close, melancholy Southerner, of decayed physique and bad blood, who haunted only the old parts of the Old World.

Paganini remains most vividly in the general mind of readers of musical history, Bull being already well-nigh unknown—even by name— to the young people of the present generation ; but Bull is, I think, better worth acquaintance, for the Norwegian was very emphatically a man of power and character, though (like Paganini) he left no school after him, and so was not permanently of importance to the art of music.

I

He was born at Bergen in 1810. His father

was a physician, whose desire was for Ole
Bornemann to study theology and enter the
Church.

There was music in the family, and much
quartet playing. Ole learnt almost instinctively
to handle the violin, though taking a few lessons
from a Dane named Paulsen and from a Swede
named Lundholm, two musicians settled at
Bergen, the latter a pupil of Baillot.

These lessons counted for little. What counted
for a good deal was the poetic folklore of the
country, which went deep into his nature, as
it went later into the nature of his countryman
Grieg, coming out constantly in his music and
giving to it a peculiar character. He was an
ardent patriot, and wherever he went in the
outside world he carried the spirit of Norway
with him—to the pride and happiness of the
Norwegians, who loved and honoured him in a
manner and to a degree we English, for example,
only find possible for soldiers and sailors.

Ole (the name is disyllabic) went to the
university to study theology. But he took his
violin with him, and spent much of his time in
conducting and directing an amateur musical
and dramatic society in Christiana, the university
town. He also spent much time in discussing
politics, which was not wise for a Norwegian,
the companion country of Sweden being the
ruling power. Perhaps for political reasons the
student of theology had to leave the city. He

certainly went away suddenly, in the year 1829, making his way to Cassel, where Spohr lived.

The young Norseman wanted to study under Spohr. But he and the German musician were antipathetic. He was of a quite different race, very animated, and indeed boisterous of manner, and (to a man like Spohr) an eccentric.

Spohr received him with coldness, and Ole Bull soon discovered that after all he could not learn of this violinist, whose views of art were so different from his own. He therefore left Cassel, went to another town, got into trouble there, as a result having to fight a duel, and returned to Norway. Thus ended Ole Bull's first journey from home.

II

Back in Bergen, he lived a musical life, playing at local concerts, until in 1831 he went back to Germany to get in touch with Paganini, who, he guessed, might help him more than Spohr. He followed Paganini to Paris. Here he observed him closely, though without taking lessons, I believe.

Having no money, and finding no opening to earn money by public performance, he fell into difficulties. For a time he more or less starved ; low spirits afflicted him, and when the added misfortune came of contact with robbers, who stripped him of all he owned, including his violin, he thought the end had come.

OLE BULL

Either out of the desperate determination to commit suicide, or by accident, he fell into the Seine, and was nearly drowned. They got him out of the river in time, and as animation was restored, so his fortune changed : a rich widow lady, into whose house he was carried, saw in his face some remote resemblance to the son she had recently lost by death ; she was drawn to him, and adopted him ; there was, moreover, a daughter in the family, destined by fate to become the young man's wife.

This lady found the means for Ole Bull to resume his musical life. A public concert was given (April 18th, 1832), in which Chopin and Heinrich Wilhelm Ernst (1814-1865), the violinist, took part ; and eventually, in 1834, when twenty-four years old, the Norwegian set off for Italy.

He had practised hard, striving to master Paganini's manner of playing, and was admitted to be an exceptionally fine performer of that kind. But success in Italy was not immediate. And he hindered matters by unwise conversation on political subjects the moment he reached Milan, which closed that town to him. A moderate success was won in Bologna, but in Rome he had no opportunities, and in Naples he had to wait six or eight months before an engagement came. This, when it arrived, established him : it was to play the violin at a theatre between the acts of a dramatic performance ; and his work was so excellent and pleasing that all the doors in Italy were at once opened for him.

III

Ole Bull now played in various Italian towns, sending his fame before him into Paris and London. It was in May, 1836, that he reached England, heralded by the journalists in the following manner, which indicates exactly his public position, the quality of his fame, and the prevailing attitude of music-lovers to musicians of the virtuoso type. He was this year twenty-six, and five years had passed since Paganini's visit.

Ole Bull, of Norway, the celebrated violinist, has arrived from Paris, and intends giving a series of concerts. His rehearsal took place yesterday. The principal feature in his playing lies in producing novel effects upon the instrument. The Parisians, who exist by wondering, say that he produces five sounds upon four strings. He really *is* a prodigy.—*Musical World*, May 6th, 1836.

Ole Bull. A man is no real *genius* in the estimation of the million, whose personal history is not connected with a considerable portion of romance. If the contour of his life, character, and behaviour be not flourished over with the arabesque of eccentricity, but little interest will be created in his favour . . . to become the observed of all men—the " digito monstror " of the multitude, his life must have a touch of the romantic. He *must* be the genius of adventure and misfortune : he must have sailed into the arctic and the antarctic of prosperity and wretchedness . . . while a casual admixture of crime will be a lucky hit. . . . Paganini, as a great artist, raised but a small commotion in the curious world ; as a dungeon-bird, however, he set the whole bevy of gossips cackling . . . he was said to be haunted by his evil conscience ; hence his mortified aspect : he had been for years immured in his solitary cell ; hence his accomplishment upon the renowned one string—the rest having worn out and broken.

The rival to Paganini, who is now causing such a flutter here in the circles, is likewise said—and, for his fame, fortunately said—to be a romantic character. He is said to have endured the extremes of good and ill-luck ; and his genius is in consequence at a premium. He is said to have been stripped to his skin— even to the purloining of his fiddle ; and all are on tiptoe of expectation. He is said to have been snatched from the extremity of desperation ; and folks are desirous of con-templating what had so narrowly escaped them. He is said to have been casting the pearls of his talent in the beastly streets of Paris ; and every concert lounger is fainting to hear him In short, he is " an interesting creature "— the true stuff to make a drawing-room lion of. His feeling, his expression, his execution, real, and profound, and astonishing as they are, become more attractive from the adventitious circumstance of his romantic life. There is probably just as much truth in the idle reports that are circulating respecting this admirable musician, as in those which preceded the arrival of Paganini : and like that sagacious person, our present visitor will laugh at them, while they are turning to his account.—*Ib.*, May 13th, 1836.

The Norwegian did well in England. In the sixteen months following May 21st, he played at 274 concerts in England, and musicians, the public, and the press were kind to him. They liked his " genuine and unaffected simplicity." His fine body, tall, and strongly built, his fair hair and clear healthy complexion, pleased all who saw him. One writer of the time observed in Ole Bull a partial resemblance to Henry Kirke White, the young poet who had now been dead thirty years ; but as this observer remarked that " his eye is small, restless, and very animated when he warms to his subject," while other writers say that his eyes were large, steady, and blue in the way of the Norsemen, we need not

OLE BULL

consider that the musician looked like that poor consumptive poet of twenty-one.

It is said by some writers of the history of those times that Ole Bull was vain, that he was quick to suspect a slight and to show annoyance, by which he made many enemies and retained few friends. This may be true or not. The larger deeds of his life, however, and the regard paid him after his death, indicate that vanity and suspicion could have been no more than minor flaws of his character.

IV

The musicians soon found that he had no classic power in his art. They found him monotonous, as they found Paganini ; but they admired his splendid virtuosity, his novel effects (due to thin strings and a flat bridge), and his poetic energy. This man's poetry came into the Italianized world of music much as the poetry of Grieg, a couple of generations later, came into the over-Teutonized world ; and it was equally welcome. Chiefly, I imagine, they admired his strength and masculinity, especially as the mysterious, uncanny, sickly, and ghost-like Paganini was yet fresh in their minds. . . . The violin, as I have said before, is almost the most masculine of instruments, demanding the strong hands of men.*

*The day before the present chapter was written, one of the chief of our British violinists, whose interpretation of the

MAKERS OF MUSIC

Ole Bull played only his own music and a few pieces by Paganini. He had not the high and general intelligence for the music of the masters, and was wise to leave it alone. His great show-piece was a *Polacca guerriera*, which he played probably as often as the cellist Van Biene played his *Broken Melody*, which was until he forgot it. Bull says he composed this piece, or at least invented it, while sitting alone at midnight, watching Mount Vesuvius flaming in eruption. An adagio preceded the polacca, in which was much of the poetry of the North, and Joachim said that no violinist of the middle nineteenth century possessed the poetic power to render it in the manner of Ole Bull

v

Leaving England, he wandered happily over the whole of Europe, through Belgium, France, Italy, Germany, Russia, and into Scandinavia. In 1844 he went to America, where he stayed

" mystical " music of Elgar is almost his finest work, told the author that his great hobby is boxing and that in his younger days he liked nothing better than to have the gloves on with a real prize-fighter, who would give proper prize-fighting blows, and receive the same. Intelligent observers from which body are excluded the sentimentalizing poetasters, have always seen that the violinist is a man or woman of splendid strength the reader should carefully consider Section xxxiv of A. C. Benson's *The Thread of Gold*, in which comes the following passage ' . . . his wonderful hands, not delicate or slender, but full strong, and muscular, moving neither lingeringly nor hastily, but with a firm and easy deliberation upon the strings. . . .''

for two years. Then he went to Algeria, and thence to Paris, living in Paris during 1847 and 1848.

From Paris he went to Bergen, after a long absence, making his home there from 1848 to 1852. He set about establishing a national theatre in the town ; and as his efforts were in some way illegal, the town authorities brought an action against him, and he was compelled to pay a heavy fine. This resulted in much pain and quarrelling ; and the violinist made his way to America again.

He took with him sad thoughts of the poverty of his fellow countrymen. The New World seemed the place for them, and he bought a large piece of land (some 125,000 acres), on which to establish a Norwegian colony. But he had bought from rogues of the kind described in " Martin Chuzzlewit." The land did not belong to the sellers, and Ole Bull was ruined.

More hard work, and more constant travelling, brought money to him again, some of which he lost in trying to establish an academy of music in Christiana. Altogether this man seems to have been one of those absurd persons who try to do good, at the ridiculous cost of emptying their own pockets.

The visits to America numbered five. The last of these was at the very end of his life, and he died a few months after his return to Norway, on his estate a few miles out of Bergen.

This was in 1880. All the Norwegians loved and honoured him, and were proud of him. The peasants came to the funeral, travelling in some cases a hundred miles; each brought a flower, or a fern, or the green bough of a tree, to heap on the grave of the man who had played their tunes to the music-lovers of the outer world.

Grieg, a native of Bergen, whose parents had been told by Ole Bull to let their son be a musician, was there, to say over the coffin, " Because more than any other thou wast the glory of our land, and hast carried our people with thee to the clear heights of art; because thou wast the pioneer of our national music, and the faithful, warm-hearted conqueror of the hearts of men, and hast planted a seed that shall spring in the future, causing the generations of the future to bless thee, I lay this laurel wreath on thy coffin, in the name of the musical art of Norway."

A still more comprehensive eulogy was pronounced by Björnstjerne Björnson, the Norwegian poet and dramatist, of which one phrase rings with great power : " He always felt himself our representative, and if he felt there was need, be it at home or abroad, that *Ole Olsen Viol, Norse Norman from Norway*, should appear, he never failed us."

Here was the ending of the first great violinist of Scandinavia, who with Paganini is sometimes called a charlatan, but was a patriot, and a son of his land and time no less than Bach in Thurin-

114

gia. He added nothing to art, but much to the lives of the people of his own country. And though he is forgotten in the world we belong to, he is, I expect, traditional among the peasantry of Norway. His influence may not cease to be direct for many generations, as Grieg said ; and this means that from him flows some little stream into the mighty river of that art which had its main rise in Corelli and Tartini.

II. PIANISTS

To ADRIAN C. BOULT

XI.   THE CLAVIERS

I

THE following pages contain the story of the
clavierists and first pianists. The story is outlined only. If given in full, it would go into
some curious byways of musical history, dis-
covering afresh men and music that have been
forgotten ; it would explain mechanism and
technique, which are highly scientific matters,
requiring diagrams, acoustics, mathematics, and
much musical type ; and it would incorporate
the substance of the entire history of music.

The latter would be a vital condition of the
story, because the keyed instrument of strings,
whether plucked or struck, has borrowed and
adapted to its own ends every characteristic of
the music of every generation. Clavierists have
learned from opera, from the church, the choir,
the solo singer, the violinist, the organist, the
full orchestra, the ballet, and everything else.
The only quality of music which the later piano
has failed to bring within its world is the lyrical
recitative ; composers have tried to adapt this,
but with no real success (except for the performer
and listener possessed of a curiously delicate
imagination) ; Bach, of course, writing for the
expressive clavichord, made use of *recitative,*
as in the Chromatic Fantasia and Fugue, and we
find that his music in this kind is still very
movingly beautiful on the piano ; but otherwise
the reservation obtains. Yet. as I have said,

it is the only reservation ; and we can regard the claviers as a mirror which reflects the art of music during the three hundred or so years of their existence.

Until the time of Beethoven, clavierists had no public position like that held by singers and violinists. And the art of *pianoforte* playing dates from the end of the eighteenth century, when the first group of the virtuosos came into being.

This art is thus recent, for the reason that the pianoforte itself did not become a reliable instrument until after the middle of the eighteenth century. Silbermann, a German, managed to satisfy Bach that there was something in the " forte-piano " ; but Mozart was the first great musician to care for the piano, and Beethoven's earlier sonatas were as much designed for the other keyed instruments as for the " hammer-clavier." Beethoven, however, was a mighty pianist, whom we are to regard as a virtuoso of the highest order in the days before Liszt : he could play, correctly and adequately, his own compositions for keyed instruments ; and it is by his writings for the piano that we of a later generation are able to realize the executive technique of a pianist-composer.

All the great composers from Bach and Handel to Brahms were clavier virtuosos, excepting Berlioz and Wagner.

THE CLAVIERS

II

There were two stringed instruments played by keys in the days before the piano. In the Harpsichord the string was plucked by a plectrum. In the Clavichord the string was made to sound by a tangent which struck it and then pushed vibratingly against it.

The plectrum, or "jack," of the harpsichord left the string the moment it had performed its operation. Thus the tone was short, a legato or a sostenuto being impossible. The touch being unalterable, the sound was uniform ; and so this instrument was provided with a swell, that is, the strings were enclosed in a box which opened at the will of the player, causing the tone to swell or diminish in volume. The harpsichord was also made with two keyboards and two sets of strings, one quieter than the other.

The player kept his fingers bent and pointing vertically to the keys in order to effect the sharp touch that made the mechanism operate completely ; after striking a key he withdrew his finger by bending it in towards the palm. The more crisp the touch, the finer the effect. The harpsichordist used his thumb, but did not pass it under the other fingers when playing a scale.

The tone of the larger harpsichords was full, bold, and penetrating ; and the instrument was used by the director of concerted music to give

121

MAKERS OF MUSIC

time and accent and to hold the performers together. The *maestro al cembalo* at Italian opera in the eighteenth century stood for our present-day conductor.

In England the instrument of harpsichord type was called the Virginals in Queen Elizabeth's time. Afterwards it was generally called the Spinet.

The tangent of the clavichord remained against its string as long as the key was depressed. By balancing his finger on the key the player could communicate a curiously individual expression to the sound, to which the name *Bebung* was given. He could vary tone and accent by the pressure of his fingers, and so the parts of a fugue could be kept distinct. Everything, however, was so quiet and delicate that in the smaller instruments only two or three persons could hear the sound distinctly*, and, of course, there was nothing sparkling or brilliant in the music. Bach wrote much of his clavier music for the clavichord, preferring it to the harpsichord when playing for his own pleasure.

The clavichordist played with the three long fingers, using a gentle pressure, and passing one finger over another in the performance of scales.

* If tne story is true of the child Handel learning to play at midnight in an attic, and if (as was most likely) the instrument he used was a clavichord, the sound of his playing would never have aroused the other folk in the house. (The familiar picture of this incident represents, in error, an instrument as big as a grand piano.)

THE CLAVIERS

We wonder how they managed to play some of their music, seeing that this is hard enough for us with the five fingers in use. The greater part of early clavier music, however, whether for harpsichord or clavichord, is in two parts only.

III

The first clavierists were generally—indeed, invariably—organists as well ; and the first clavier music was but a pale copy of music in organ style.

The history of clavier music is the record of a slow discovery of the right manner of playing, and thus of writing for, the instrument.

And when the piano was first used, composers for a while wrote for it in the manner of the earlier claviers. The fine pianoforte manner of to-day dates from Liszt, Chopin, and Schumann. Mozart, however, who took to the piano about the middle of his life, was delighted to find that the works he had written for harpsichord went just as well on the piano.

Chief among the great organist-clavierist musicians of the early seventeenth century is Girolamo Frescobaldi (1583-1644), an Italian who attracted an audience of thirty thousand persons when playing the organ in Rome in the year 1614. Two English contemporaries of his were William Byrd (1543-1623) and John Bull (1563-1628), the latter a man who lived abroad

MAKERS OF MUSIC

a good deal. A German contemporary was Samuel Scheidt (1587-1654).

The English clavierists from William Byrd to Orlando Gibbons (1583-1625) were far in advance of Frescobaldi and the other Continental performers. Not only was their music clearer, more characteristic, and stronger, but their instrumental technique was more individual. The music they wrote for the virginals is almost as unlike the music they wrote for voices as is the harpsichord music of Scarlatti, born a hundred years later. While Frescobaldi was still thinking in terms of the organ though writing for the clavier, and while his actual music was very primitive, so that it means next to nothing to us to-day, Byrd, Bull, and Gibbons had discovered keyboard qualities that have never left instrumental music, being essentially true to the keyboard ; and their music is so fresh and living that it is still played by pianists in public.

The student will one day learn William Byrd's variations on *The Carman's Whistle*, John Bull's *The King's Hunt Jigg*, and the *Fantasia of Four Parts* by Orlando Gibbons.

Of clavierists born in the seventeenth century, the student should carry in mind Froberger, Johann Kaspar Kerll, Georg Böhm, Johann Krieger, Franz Xaver Murschhauser, Johann Kuhnau, Johann Pachelbel, and Alessandro Poglietti, in addition to the great masters Bach, Handel and Scarlatti.

THE CLAVIERS

The only way to learn anything of value regarding these early musicians is to examine some of their music. The student is therefore recommended to buy a volume of music entitled *Alte Meister des Klavierspiels*, which is No. 3173 of the Edition Peters. This collection makes a survey of all clavier music up to the end of the 18th century, omitting Bach, Handel, Haydn, Mozart, Hasse, Bach's sons, and a few other composers whose works are available in popular editions.

A piano student able to play Bach and Beethoven will not find any of the pieces difficult of those in the Peters volume ; and a summer vacation is pleasantly filled by working through the collection.

XII. FROBERGER, MARCHANI SCARLATTI

FROBERGER, THE GERMAN

JOHANN JACOB FROBERGER, who died in 1667, is the first man we can select here to illustrate the character and life of the earlier masters of the clavier. He is not remote in time, for he belongs to the same generation as Milton ; but he persists in remaining a dim figure, as if a member of some remote civilization.

This is because we know little of his music, and because no writer of the time has given us an account of Froberger by which we can see the man at work and observe the nature of his mind. The chief story told of him is not altogether authentic. We are ignorant of his childhood ; even the date of his birth is obscure to the extent of at least twenty years, and as a result we do not know if he died old or only middle-aged. Taking him all in all, Froberger typifies the dimness of the dawn of this new art.

He is one of a group of musicians called the Germanic-Roman School. These are Germans who, having studied under the great Roman composers, were influenced by them, blending with the rich Teutonic qualities of their native musicianship some of the purer, more severe qualities of Roman art. Frescobaldi and Carissimi were the chief of these Italians : the Germans they attracted had, for the most part, already done work with Italians in other centres, in particular Venice, where song and opera prevailed ; and so the Germanic-Venetian-Roman musicians were among the best equipped of all in their time.

The German and Austrian rulers and nobles who maintained a good musical establishment, sent clever young musicians to study in Italy, now as for the next two hundred years.   It was by the Emperor of Austria that Froberger was sent to Frescobaldi.

For a long time it was thought Froberger was born in 1635.   But it has been discovered that in 1637 he was organist to the court at Vienna. And then, when it was found that, according to one record, he was turned sixty at the time of his death, in 1667, the date of his birth was moved back to 1605.   But if born in 1605, he was thirty-two when sent by the Emperor to study in Italy, which would be a very advanced age for such a distinction.   The clever young Germans rarely travelled south later than the age of twenty or twenty-two.

You may consider that Froberger was born about 1612, which was some forty years earlier than Corelli.

Halle, in Saxony, the native town of Handel, was his birthplace.   His father, it is believed, was town cantor.   The boy was a youthful

prodigy, locally famous for his playing of the
organ and cembalo, and eminent official visitors
to the town (some say the Swedish Ambassador
to Austria) discovered him and sent him with
recommendations to the Austrian court.

He was the first German clavierist to become
famous throughout Europe. His years in Rome
ran from 1637 to 1641. During that period he
either visited Paris or became acquainted with
French musicians, because his clavier music is
marked by those "agréments" (trills, turns,
mordents, and other ornamental touches) which
are characteristic of the French clavicinists of the
time.

These decorations belong entirely to the
old clavier ; they serve to mark accent and to
effect an artificial sustaining of the tone, and as
they are not wanted on the piano, we can omit
the bulk of them.

Bach studied Froberger's music carefully,
as he did the work of every great musician
before him. How worthy of Bach's study it
was can be gathered from the following, which is
the opening of a sarabande :

FROBERGER.

Among the pieces copied by the child Bach by moonlight, while living with his brother (see *Masters of Music*, page 77), were works by this composer, who thus came to the knowledge of John Sebastian at the earliest moment possible. As Froberger's musical script was clear as engraving, he probably set the pattern of that beautiful manner of writing music for which Bach is notable.

Froberger used to decorate the pages of his manuscript with little figures and florid arabesques. The copies he presented to patrons he had bound in the finest leather, richly tooled in gold. Not much music was printed in those days, and none of Froberger's existed in his lifetime but in manuscript.

He held office under the Austrian emperor until 1657 ; but his attendance becoming more and more erratic, the emperor at last dismissed him. He then found a patron in the Duchess Sybilla of Würtemburg, in whose palace he eventually died.

According to the story, Froberger undertook a journey to London in 1662, when he would be about fifty years old. He travelled through France. Before reaching the coast he was attacked by robbers, who stripped him of all his possessions, leaving him only his under-garments and a few coins secreted next his skin. Reaching Calais in rags, yet with a cheerful spirit, he took passage on a ship to England.

Pirates boarded the ship when it was within a mile or two of the English coast, and Froberger, to escape the general slaughter, leapt overboard. Being a strong swimmer (and for certain not a man sixty years old) he managed to struggle to land—either this, or he had the good fortune to be picked up by a boat. Some fisherfolk took pity on him, gave him a few clothes, and showed him the road to London, which he walked begging his way.

Arrived in London, weary, destitute, and by

now very miserable, he went into Westminster
Abbey to rest, pray, and listen to the organ
music which had floated out to him in the street.
The old organist, Christopher Gibbons, was
playing to himself in the dusk of the evening.

Froberger sank into a profound reverie, until
he was aroused by the organist coming to the
door, which he had to lock after him. The two
men got into conversation.

" You seem unfortunate," said Gibbons.

" I am, indeed, the child of misfortune,"
said Froberger. " Robbers and pirates have
brought me to this pass. I have no money, no
food, and I know not where I shall sleep."

He did not say who he was. But Gibbons,
happening to be in want of an organ-blower,
offered him the work if food and clothes would
serve as payment ; an offer which Froberger
was happy to accept. He had lost his credentials,
and guessed it was no good trying to introduce
himself to the court of King Charles ; but fancied
that his association with the Abbey organist—
who was also court organist—might afford him
an opportunity to reveal himself.

And so it turned out. On May 21st, Charles
the Second and Catherine of Portugal were
married. In the course of the festivals, Gibbons
was playing the organ to the court, Froberger
blowing by his side. Lost in thought as he
watched the court crowd, he let the wind out of
the organ just as Gibbons was arriving at the

climax of his piece. This enraged the old man. He cursed the blower, and left the chapel.

There was a general surprise ; but Froberger saw his opportunity : he filled the bellows, slipped on to the stool, and, drawing a few light stops, extemporized in most masterly fashion. In the crowd was a lady who had studied under Froberger in Vienna. She recognized her master in the playing. Speaking to the King, she was commanded to bring this mysterious stranger into the royal presence. A harpsichord was sent for, and Froberger there and then played for an hour to the King and his companions. Immediately he was a royal favourite, and everything was bright and pleasant.

Froberger himself tells this story, and we may as well believe it true as false.

He died five years later. The Duchess Sybilla raised a monument to his memory, and in a letter to Christian Huygens, said : " I am left alone (may God grant me His grace !), a poor and humble pupil of my dear, honest, faithful, and industrious teacher, the good Master Johann Jacob Froberger."

II

LOUIS MARCHAND, THE FRENCHMAN

A year after Froberger's death was born François Couperin (1668-1733), who was the chief French clavierist of his time, and the first great composer of true harpsichord music. He stands in the history of this instrument much as Corelli and Tartini stand in the history of the violin.

His works were re-issued in the nineteenth century, edited by Brahms. Many of them are little pictorial sketches, and we still play them in our work at the piano.

Couperin, however, is not in the history of the clavier so important a man as the Italian Domenico Scarlatti, of whom I shall speak when I have described Louis Marchand, the first unpleasant individual among clavier virtuosos.

This Louis Marchand, born in 1669, died 1732, was a fine organist and clavierist, and a good musician generally. He was organist of several churches in Paris, and court organist to the King. (Couperin was the king's chamber musician, or clavicinist.)

But he was a proud and dissipated man. And his pride was such as makes a man think he is indispensable, out of which error he acts recklessly. Thus the King hearing that Marchand neglected his wife so badly that often she was actually without food, gave directions that half his salary should be withheld and paid directly to Madame Marchand ; upon which Marchand, at the service of the Mass next following this arrangement, left the organ before the Agnus Dei. It was thought he was ill, and no special attention was paid to the matter ; but when an hour later the King saw him strolling about the grounds of the palace, and was informed by Marchand that if his wife had half the money, she must do half the work, the King ordered him out of the country.

Marchand went into Germany, carrying his impertinence with him. He was well received at the King of Poland's court, which was then established in Dresden, and his musical ability was recognized. But his arrogant pride, and especially his sneers at German music, musicians, and musicianship, set people against him. He was constantly saying he could play any German organist or clavierist off the map ; and at last this general challenge, so graciously and modestly expressed, was accepted.

He was certainly a fine performer, and only one man was available with the ability to put him in second place. This was young Sebastian Bach, now in the service of the Duke of Weimar. The Dresdeners enquired secretly of B ch if he would come and compete with this Frenchman, and Bach said he would. They enquired secretly because it was their desire to catch Marchand in the height of his pride, so that his defeat should be the more galling.

The plot was laid, with the King's knowledge and consent. A court concert was held, at which Marchand played brilliantly a set of variations he had recently written on a French song. There was much applause. Then one of the plotters asked permission that a German player, who happened to be in the town, and was present in the room, should be asked to show his skill, in the hope that native art might show itself not without credit in the company of this wonderful Frenchman. Permission received, young Bach came to the clavier, the while Marchand waited with that air for which the Germans loved him. To his surprise, the quiet and grave German, after a short prelude, actually played the set of variations which Marchand had just given out for the first time in public ; and then, heaping injury on insult, the German followed with another set, all extemporaneous, which infinitely surpassed the first in all the qualities of variety, energy, and brilliance.

But the game was not yet finished. In the midst of his mortification, Marchand was reminded of his offer to play against any German organist, as well as against any German clavierist ; and Bach wrote down a theme for him to study overnight, undertaking to meet the Frenchman the next day, when he would play extemporaneously on any theme Marchand cared to suggest.

To save his face, Marchand agreed to the meeting. But when the next day came, he was not to be found. He had run away.

Eventually the French king allowed the man to return to Paris. Here he became again the

MAKERS OF MUSIC

most fashionable and expensive of teachers, able
to earn several pounds a day. But his dissipation
kept him poor, and he died in extreme misery.
Towards the end of his life he developed jealousy
of any pupil who displayed particular ability. He
was especially vindictive towards his pupil
Rameau.

III

DOMENICO SCARLATTI, THE ITALIAN

The climax in the art of the harpsichord was
achieved by Domenico Scarlatti, who was born
either in 1685, the year when Bach and Handel
were born, or in 1683. He died in 1757, two
years before Handel, and seven after Bach.

This art suffered a decline in the generation
following Scarlatti, while the art of the pianoforte was gradually rising. When—seventy
years later than Scarlatti—Beethoven died in
Vienna, the new art was nearly perfected, requiring only the work of Chopin and Liszt.

Bach, as we know, was a great clavierist.
Handel, according to one story, was as great a
player in his young manhood as Scarlatti. Yet
Scarlatti, more clearly than any other, appears
the prince of harpsichordists. We play the bulk
of Bach's clavier music as if it were piano music
of a pre-Beethoven type. A few of Handel's
works for clavier we play in the same manner.

136

DOMENICO SCARLATTI

But Scarlatti's music, although we have to use it on our instrument of hammers, we invariably remember to be harpsichord music ; and it is the only pure harpsichord music regularly in use in our new world of the piano—just as Scarlatti is the only early clavierist whose influence on playing can be traced (through Clementi and Czerny) to Mendelssohn and Liszt and Albeniz.

Frescobaldi for the organ ; Corelli for the violin ; and Scarlatti for the harpsichord. These are the three men always to be remembered in connection with the three instruments ; and they were men of successive generations.

Domenico's father was the great Alessandro Scarlatti, one of the masters of Neapolitan opera. He was his son's first teacher. The second was Francesco Gasparini (or, Guasparini), a violinist, cembalist, and composer, associated with Corelli.

This Gasparini did much to remove harpsichord playing from its dependence on organ playing, introducing more freely trills, running scales, sweeping arpeggios, and the like. The cembalist who worked in operatic performances had to play from a figured bass (that is, a single line of music, with figures indicating the harmonies) ; and Gasparini's " Method of Thorough-Bass Playing " was the chief textbook on the subject from 1683 to 1802, in which last year it reached its seventh edition.

Alessandro Scarlatti was a typical Neapolitan—

warm-blooded, inventive, and intellectually active. Domenico was the same, despite the severe and scholarly face shown in portraits ; but he was not, in music, emotional or sentimental, and could not have written the broad music of Froberger, shown on page 128.

For some years Domenico was a writer of operas. There was no other means of making a livelihood in Italy at that time ; and the harpsichord, unlike the violin and the voice, was not much in favour. And in general it may be said that the Italians have never cared much for the clavier, whether harpsichord, clavichord, or pianoforte.

As his particular gifts had no scope in Naples, his father sent him to Venice, directing him on no account to settle in Rome, where the art of harpsichord music, a beggar in Naples, would certainly find no shelter. It was in 1705 that Domenico left home. In a letter to the Duke of Florence, Alessandro said : " This son of mine is an eagle whose wings are grown ; he should not remain idle in the nest, nor should I hinder his flight."

In Venice Domenico met an Englishman named Thomas Rosingrave (Roseingrave), who is deserving a moment's thought here as a good representative English player on the harpsichord.

Rosingrave (1690-1768) belonged to a family of musicians who did good work in the seventeenth and eighteenth centuries. He was a fine harpsi-

DOMENICO SCARLATTI

chordist, a good organist, a wonderful player from full orchestral scores, and a true master of performing from the figured bass. But there was a defect in his nature. He was over-sensitive, brooding, and inclined to melancholy ; and when, about the age of thirty-five, he met with a disappointment in love, his mind became unsettled. The girl he loved was one of his pupils. Her father was a rich man, who, of course, would not allow his daughter to marry a musician, than which there was little lower in the social scale, or, indeed, in the simple scale of respectability, in the eighteenth century. Rosingrave remained sane on all points except this of his love. When the subject was mentioned, he fell into a mild form of madness. But for the remainder of his life he neglected his work, and was often destitute.

Rosingrave and Scarlatti met in Venice in the year 1710, whither Rosingrave had gone to study, aided by a grant of ten guineas from the Dean and Chapter of St. Patrick's Cathedral, Dublin. He took such an admiration for Scarlatti that he hardly left him all the time he remained in Italy, following from town to town, as faithful a friend as may be imagined.

Rosingrave was already a well-known cembalist when he went to Venice, and his letters of introduction took him at once into the houses of the nobility. He was invited to play at an " academy " (as a private evening concert was then named), and being in good form, his courage high and fingers unusually active and strong, he played well, receiving much applause. In the room was a " grave young man dressed in black and in a black wig, who had stood in one corner of the room, very quiet and attentive while Rosingrave played." Later on the grave young man was asked to play ; and play he did, in a manner to make Rosingrave think ten hundred devils were at the instrument. (The expression is his own.) So astounding was the execution, and so bewilderingly novel the effects, that the younger man would have cut his fingers off rather than touch a harpsichord again : so he thought, and for a month after. It was in this way that Scarlatti and Rosingrave became acquainted.

The regard of Rosingrave for Scarlatti was not unlike the regard of Scarlatti for Handel. The latter was in Venice about this time. When he went to Rome, the Italian followed the Saxon, and the Irishman followed the Italian.

At Cardinal Ottoboni's house there was a contest between the two. Handel won at the organ. He and Scarlatti were adjudged equal at the harpsichord ; but for the rest of his life Scarlatti spoke with reverence of Handel's clavierism, crossing himself, as if in the presence of something sacred. Corelli would be present at this meeting.

For about ten years Domenico remained in

DOMENICO SCARLATTI

Rome. He then came to London, to supervise the production of one of his operas. Handel was here then, and Rosingrave (who was instrumental in the production) was *maestro al cembalo*.

In 1721 he was in Lisbon, where the King of Portugal tried hard to get him to remain permanently ; even granting three hundred pounds travelling expenses in his anxiety to create a good impression on the famous musician. Scarlatti taught some of the members of the royal family, forming acquaintances which eventually induced him to go to Madrid, one of his pupils becoming Queen of Spain. Italy, however, drew him again for a while ; and it was not until 1729, when he was forty-four (or forty-six) that he established himself in the service of the King of Spain.

One report is that he died here, another that he went back to Italy for the last three years of his life.

Scarlatti, we understand, was a hopeless gambler. His family, left destitute, were aided by the singer Farinelli.

Coming to the music of this virtuoso after a little acquaintance with the music of his contemporary Bach, you are surprised by its different character. Almost all the qualities you found in Bach are here wanting. There are no deep emotions, vast phrases, close contrapuntal searchings, minute accentuations, lengthy melodies, or

inexhaustible varieties. On the contrary, everything is just fresh, cheerful, vigorous and
spirited, in accordance with Scarlatti's Italian
nature, and in accordance with the nature of
the harpsichord as a solo instrument.

It was this coincidence of a mind and an
instrument in perfect accord that made Scarlatti
the supreme *harpsichordist* in musical history,
after whom no advance was possible.

His prefatory remarks to an issue of some
pieces, made when the composer was nearly
sixty years old, indicate the spirit in which his
music is to be taken. " Amateur or professor,
whoever thou art ! in these compositions seek
not a deep feeling. They are but a frolic of art,
intended to increase thy confidence on the
clavier. I had no ambition to make a sensation :
I was merely requested to publish them. If
they prove not entirely unpleasing to thee, I shall
the more willingly entertain other commissions
of like nature, to the end that I may rejoice thee
in lighter and more varied styles. Therefore,
take these present pieces rather as man than
critic, since only so shalt thou increase thine own
content. To speak of the use of the two hands—
D denotes *dritta*, the Right, and *M* denotes *manca*,
the Left. Farewell ! "

Domenico Scarlatti brought speed into performance, and that general lightness and activity
which mark piano playing. Some of his technical
features (scales in thirds and sixths, reiterated

notes, certain arpeggio shapes, and the like), were not incorporated in piano playing until fifty years after his death, so advanced was his executive art. Indeed, the first pianists, Mozart among them, objected to these features. Clementi, however, and slightly later pianists built up their art on Scarlatti ; Czerny, Liszt, and Bülow used his music and edited it for the convenience of piano students ; and as late as the year 1900 a complete edition of his works was begun, which within a few years had incorporated three or four hundred pieces.

Therefore this Italian harpsichordist is called the Father of Pianoforte Playing. His successor in the art of clavier music was a true German, one of Bach's sons, by name Carl Philipp Emanuel, whose music is not of the Italian type, but of the type represented by Haydn, Mozart, and Beethoven.

XIII. PHILIPP
EMANUEL BACH

I

J. S. Bach and the Fortepiano

The idea of combining the clavier and the dulcimer, that is, of striking the strings by hammers, not plucking them with a quill or a tangent, was brought to a practical issue by an Italian maker of harpsichords named Bartolommeo Cristofori. This was in the first decade of the eighteenth century.

The new instrument was named the " harpsichord with soft and loud "—in Italian *Gravecembalo col Piano e Forte*. The first German maker of pianos was Gottfried Silbermann (1683-1753). It took a hundred years to get the piano into shape, so many were the problems to be solved ; and the history of this matter, together with an account of the various stages in the development of piano technique and of piano music, makes interesting study. But it is not a subject to be treated of here.

Frederick the Great had several of the *fortepianos* of Silbermann ; and when Bach visited him in 1747, the King asked him to try them. Bach extemporized on one of the instruments, and played some of his clavier pieces ; and then, after praising the tone and expressing approval of the hammer principle, said that the touch was

144

too heavy and the treble register far too weak.
Silbermann, yielding to these criticisms, made no
more instruments until, after hard and careful
work, he had modified the defects.

Bach, of course, did not adopt the new instrument ; but he had only another three years to
live. And though before long the piano was
recognized, so much so that after 1770 a piece of
music would be announced as to be played on
either harpsichord or fortepiano, the fact remains
that up to the end of the century the old instrument held its place, even the first sonatas of
Beethoven being announced *pour le Clavecin ou
Piano Forte.*

Yet all through the second half of the
eighteenth century the art of clavier playing
shaped itself for the piano ; not in conscious
effort to suit the coming instrument, but in
obedience to the great laws governing the making
of the new music, with which the pianoforte is
entirely in agreement. During the past hundred
and twenty-five years this instrument has become
the most popular of all that have ever existed,
and the cause is simply this perfect fitness of the
piano to accept the music of that period. It does
not, of course, produce all that music to perfection ; but it gives a fair approximation, with
the already mentioned exception of lyrical declamation or recitative.

MAKERS OF MUSIC

II

PHILIPP EMANUEL BACH

Of the many clavierists after Scarlatti, it will serve here to speak of Carl Philipp Emanuel Bach (1714-1784), the third son of Johann Sebastian.

Philipp Emanuel was less virtuosic than Scarlatti, and less musically intellectual than his father. He was by nature too earnest to follow the simple and single path of Scarlatti, and too differently constituted from his father to attempt to write music in the old manner.

It was his desire in performance not to surprise you by executive skill, or to keep you intellectually alert ; but to make music and performance easy and natural, and to warm you, so that you and he might be mutually sympathetic. His art is lyrical in the instrumental manner ; it is brilliant enough, finely decorated, and accompanied by many varied effects ; yet it is still lyrical, and we look on him as the father of the lyrical school of clavier music.

To this lyrical school belong Haydn, Mozart, Pleyel, Vogler, Gelinek, Clementi, Steibelt, Dussek, Field, Hummel, Moscheles, Mendelssohn, Cramer, and many others whose names are well-known to the piano student.

Six of his sonatas were published by Bülow (Edition Peters, No. 276), which should be familiar to the young musician interested in the history of classical sonatas and pianoforte playing.

For nearly thirty years this Bach was accompanist to King Frederick the Great. He kept the king's favour all that while, though there were constant tussles between them, the King having an idea of time in music which Bach, being an artist, found unpleasant and difficult. But the people in Berlin thought little of him ; his music did not interest them, and for all his dignity, worth, and philosophical calm, he was not altogether happy there.

For the last twenty years of his life he lived in Hamburg, music director of an important church, and composer of much sacred music. His fame now was very wide. All the great men in European music respected him, and pupils visited him from many places. In 1753, when in his fortieth year, he had published a book on the art of clavier playing which lifted him into the front rank of critics, and which laid down principles that formed the foundation of the work of Clementi and Cramer.

Philipp Emanuel thought highly of Haydn ; he studied his music, and wrote to him. In his turn, Haydn, eighteen years the younger, thought highly of Philipp Emanuel, for he had based his own manner of music on a close study of his work. Mozart said : " He is the father, we the children ; and those of us who can do anything, we learned it of him." Even warmer was Haydn's "I owe to Carl Philipp Emanuel Bach whatever I may know or may be able to do.'' Years later, Beethoven praised him almost as highly.

He was, indeed, an admirable man ; and we ought to be told more of him in our histories, quite apart from the fact that without knowledge of his works we cannot thoroughly under-stand the story of Haydn, Mozart, and Beethoven, or the growth of the new lyrico-dramatic music. He demanded feeling in the performer, saying that if you do not feel the music you cannot convey anything to your listeners. '' We must play from the heart,'' he said, '' not in the way a trained bird sings.'' And he advocated absolute individuality in the living musician, not a thoughtless, lazy, or pedantic reliance on tradi-tion. '' For us of to-day the laws of our fathers are a confinement ; while wisdom, science, and courage admit no such restriction.'' But it was a rational liberty he advocated and practised—a liberty which is that of habit and feeling, oper-ating on known and accepted law ; not a reck-less, revolutionary exercise of uncontrolled in-dividuality, which in art as in politics makes for anarchy and ceaseless change, with nothing permanent remaining.

The majority of the critics were not his friends, because he was advanced beyond the stage of art that gave them their rules. But whoever heard him play his music, in the varying moods of vivacity and tenderness it required, became his supporters.

PHILIPP EMANUEL BACH

Towards the latter portion of his life Bach ceased to trouble about adverse criticism : " When I turned fifty I gave up all ambition. I wanted only to live in peace, and work as long as I could, not knowing how near my end might be."

He wrote several hundred works for the clavichord, of which instrument he had a fine Silbermann make. Among them are dozens of three-movement sonatas—the first movement active, vivid, and warmly emotional (in the pre-Beethoven manner, of course, which seems rather cool to us of to-day) ; the second movement more tranquil, and sometimes of interludial character ; the third happy, often impetuous, but always an intensification of the general prevailing mood of the sonata. His fingering was modern, with free use of the thumb.

Philipp Emanuel did not particularly care for the harpsichord, because it would not yield the delicate effects he desired in music. A publication of his, issued in 1781, was announced as equally for the piano as for other claviers ; but though he gave the *Fortepiano* credit for several good qualities, whether in solo or with an orchestra (provided the band were not too powerful), he still found that all the good qualities of the hammer-clavier were in his favourite instrument, allowance made for its weaker tone, and with the great additional beauty of the *bebung* and the sustained tone, neither of which existed in the

149

piano. " After striking the key, I can further press down on any note ; and the clavichord is consequently the instrument on which one can most thoroughly test [the musicianship of] a clavierist."

The slight balancing of the finger which created the *bebung* persisted as a mannerism among pianists for nearly a hundred years, though in the nature of things it would have no effect on the tone, the hammer leaving the string the moment the sound was made ; and twenty years ago middle-aged pianists who, in childhood, had been trained by very old musicians still let their hand roll a little while holding down a long note, for all the world like a 'cellist playing an expressive melody.

XIV. MOZART AND
CLEMENTI

I

Mozart took to the pianoforte in 1777, when he was twenty-one. Having already been a clavierist for seventeen or eighteen years, with knowledge of playing in many countries, this conversion was not hasty, but the outcome of much experience and observation.

He was at Augsburg that year, where lived Georg Andreas Stein, a famous maker of organs and claviers, and now of pianos. Thirty years had passed since Bach tried Silbermann's forte-pianos in the palace at Potsdam ; and the instrument, successively and independently improved by a number of makers, had become worthy the musician. Mozart was delighted with the swift tone—also with the equally swift cutting-off of the tone when the key was released. The easy action pleased him. The grander quality of the sound, with its fuller volume, brought out finely the energetic substance of his music ; and for the remainder of his life he elected to play on and compose for the piano. (We are not, however, to imagine that the piano tone heard by Mozart was nearly so large as that we ourselves hear from instruments of the present day.)

Writing in October, 1777, he says : "My last sonata, in D, comes out inimitably on the Stein pianoforte." (This would be the work containing the Rondeau en Polonaise and—for finale—the Tema con Variazioni.)

The people in Mannheim and other towns, where the piano was largely is use among amateurs, declared that they had never heard anyone touch the instrument so delicately as Mozart, and he seems to have been hailed as the first true virtuoso of the pianoforte. Clementi, however, was alive, and by four years the senior of Mozart ; but he did not begin to travel until 1781.

Mozart did not care for his piano music to be taken over-fast.

II

Muzio Clementi (1752-1832) was the first musician to devote himself to the art of the piano theoretically, scientifically, and practically. He was a great player in the Scarlattian manner, but remains in mind chiefly as teacher and writer of studies.

This Italian was more closely connected with England than any other country, dying on his estate near Evesham, a little country town less than thirty miles from Birmingham.

He was born in Rome. The family had some musical interests, and Muzio showed that he had ability when but a few years old. The father, a goldsmith or silversmith, was glad to let the boy study ; and Muzio won, after

MOZART AND CLEMENTI

competition, a position as church-organist when only nine years old. Five years later a Mass of his was sung, making him famous in the city.

He had already begun to specialize in clavier playing and without doubt he wanted to leave home for France or Germany, where that art was better appreciated than in Rome ; but the father preferred that he should stay in Italy, living the safe life of teacher and organist, with a good post as theatre harpsichordist for final goal. However, an Englishman appeared, who was struck with Muzio's cleverness ; and after long discussions the goldsmith allowed him to adopt his son, and to take him away to England.

This man was Peter Beckwith, a Member of Parliament, whose family was highly placed, including among its members soldiers, administrators, and literary folk. He had an estate in Dorsetshire, where the young Italian lived until 1770, carrying on his musical studies and perfecting his clavier technique.

Clementi's mind was like Domenico Scarlatti's. He was very strong, non-sentimental, of splendid energy, quickly working intellect, and fiery temperament. The general animation of his nature remained with him to the end of his life ; and when he was nearly eighty he used to delight pianists of the standing of Moscheles ; though by then his style was antiquated, as it had been for thirty years.

During those years in Dorsetshire he worked

at the music of Bach, Handel, Scarlatti,
Paradies, and other musicians of the century,
and wrote many pieces for the piano ; but among
these were very few slow movements.

He came up to London in 1770, the year
Beethoven was born, and was established as a
great performer the moment he had given one
or two concerts in public. Here he stayed ten
years busy with teaching and composing, acting
as cembalist-conductor at the Italian opera
for the period from 1777 to 1780.

In 1781 he left for his first long tour on the
Continent, which extended from Paris to Vienna.

III

People were still fond of competitions, as
they were for another fifty years, and nothing
delighted them more than to get two famous
players in the same room and to excite them to
mutual emulation. The pianists themselves
enjoyed the contests. They would even play
duets together. Nowadays we never see two
great virtuosos of the piano at the same music-
making ; consequently the mass of duet-music
written in the classical period is not heard in
public.*

*Once, in 1868, George Henschel was at one of Liszt's Sunday
At-Homes, and there he heard play Anton Rubinstein, Carl
Tausig, Hans von Bülow, and Liszt ; so that, in a small private
room, and by immediate impression, he could compare " the
stupendous power of a Rubinstein with the polished infallibility

MOZART AND CLEMENTI

Mozart and Clementi being in Vienna together, the Emperor suggested a competition. The two musicians agreed, and there was much local excitement.

Clementi's fame had run before him. Mozart was famous, both as a composer and as a pianist. The two had already met. But when Clementi first caught sight of Mozart, he thought he must be one of the court chamberlains, so elegantly was he dressed, and so precise was his manner, though his eye was restlessly active and his manner was abstracted. Clementi had also met Haydn.

It was Mozart's enemies who suggested to the Emperor that the pianists should play one against the other. These enemies were the members of the Italian party of Viennese musicians, who welcomed the advent of the Italian pianist, Clementi, having little doubt he would scotch Mozart's growing fame as a performer. No other musician in the place could stand against Mozart in any department of his art, but this does not mean he was in a secure and respected position.

of a Tausig, the irreproachable classicism of a Bülow with the enchanting grace and romanticism of a Liszt." Such meetings of the giants of the art were not infrequent up to fifty years ago. In Vienna you could, at a private party a century ago, hear Beethoven, Czerny, and half a dozen others. To-day, however, you can hear half the masters of the world in one evening on the "Duo-Art" pianola piano or the Steinway-Welte reproducing piano; and thus you have at least the substance of their art, if not the present personality of the men themselves.

155

Mozart prepared himself for the contest by practising, which was an exercise he did not often take.

Clementi played first. He gave a prelude, the well-known sonata in B flat, and the almost equally familiar toccata. This last was the supreme exhibition of his virtuosity ; and it was a novelty, in that running scales in thirds were not at that time frequent in music. Mozart disliked the effect of these scales.

After Clementi had finished, Mozart preludized, and then played a set of variations. The contest so far was so close that the audience could not declare either the victor ; but I expect that Mozart was the better, and that if the Italian musicians had been excluded he would have been pronounced such.

Now came the last and greatest attempt of all, in which not only technique but the quick eye and mind were required. This was sightplaying, the piece a sonata by Paesiello, " in a miserable manuscript of his own," as Mozart said in a letter to his father. The German took the opening allegro, the Italian the andante and rondo, and again each was declared the equal of the other.

Lastly came an extemporized duet. This was managed by one player being *primo* at one moment, the other being *secondo*, with occasional changing over, so that the original accompanying member of the pair became leader.

MOZART AND CLEMENTI

The one leading had the choice of theme. . .
We wonder how earlier musicians managed to
extemporize duets, until we recollect that, after
all, the material of music in the early classical
period was fairly stereotyped, in harmony,
melody, shape of phrase, rhythms, figures, and
accent, and that a man of quick mind could
see the course of a phrase almost as soon as it
was started.

In this third portion of the entertainment
honours were again left equal.

Mozart's fee for the evening was fifty ducats,
or a couple of guineas. (He used to receive
five shillings for a lesson.)

Clementi praised his opponent's playing. He
said that never before had he heard so pure a
lyrical art on the piano, or observed such ease,
grace, and charm. Mozart thought little of
Clementi's work:—

Now about this Clementi. He possesses
considerable execution, and when you have
said this you have said everything. He has a
brilliant right hand, and his principal passages
are thirds ; but in other respects, not a farthing's
worth of taste or feeling—a mere mechanic. . . .
Though I had borrowed for myself Countess
Thun's pianoforte, I played on it only when
performing alone, as the Emperor so desired
it. The other pianoforte was out of tune, and
had three of its keys sticking down. "It is

of no consequence," said the Emperor. . . .
Thus Mozart to his father.

Dittersdorf records in his autobiography a
long conversation with this Emperor, in which
comes a reference to Clementi and Mozart :

Emperor (still more gravely) : H'm ! Your
answers are direct enough

I (in a tone of deep respect) : I have been
taught that Your Majesty expects short,
concise, and unvarnished answers. If I am
mistaken, I ask your pardon.

Emperor (more gently) : You have been
taught correctly, and your answers have not
offended me. (*Then, after a short pause, and
with his former air of condescension :*) Have
you heard Mozart play ?

I : Three times already.

Emperor : Do you like him ?

I : Yes ; all musicians do.

Emperor : You have heard Clementi, too ?

I : Yes.

Emperor : Some prefer him to Mozart,
and Greybig is at the head of them. What
do you think ? Out with it !

I : Clementi's playing is art simply and
solely ; Mozart's combines art and taste.

Emperor : I say the same. You and I seem
to have taken a leaf out of the same book.

I : That we have ; and, what is more, out of
the great book—Experience.

MOZART

MOZART AND CLEMENTI

Emperor : What do you think of Mozart's compositions ?

I : He is, without question, one of the greatest musical geniuses. . . .

Emperor : He has one only fault in his pieces for the stage, and his singers have very often complained of it—he deafens them with his full accompaniment. . . .

Mozart was the most popular pianist in Vienna for five years after the competition with Clementi.

IV

Returning to England, Clementi lived in London from 1782 to 1802, with one visit to Paris in 1785. He made a fortune, which he lost in a business. Then he established a piano factory, in which to make the stronger and firmer instrument that English and French pianists preferred above the light Viennese piano. This second venture made him a rich man.

In 1802 Clementi travelled abroad again, taking with him his pupil John Field. In due course they arrived at Petersburg, where Field remained, very thankful to be free of his master—as will be told later. Returning to Berlin, Clementi spent some time teaching, among his pupils being Berger, Klengel, Moscheles, and Kalkbrenner. In 1804 he married a young girl,

L

who died the following year while they were in Italy. Another visit to Russia, this time with Berger and Klengel, who likewise elected to remain permanently in Petersburg and Moscow ; and then Clementi came home to England, in 1810, not to leave the country again.

After 1806 he developed a more singing style of performance. In 1817 he issued his famous *Gradus ad Parnassum.*

Clementi was not a poet-musician, but an inventor, explorer, and administrator in the sphere of piano playing. He does not seem to have been interested in music as music. Beethoven, however, admired the clear logic of his forms and his precise, economical expression, keeping some of his works in his small library. Czerny did not care for them.

The world was filled with Clementi's pupils, and it has been calculated that in the course of his long life half the good pianists of Europe passed through his hands. He himself played with entire equality of tone, and invented those exercises which are still used to strengthen the weak fingers. He kept the back of the hand flat, and it was he who hit on that distracting, heartbreaking custom of placing a penny on a pupil's hand, in order to show what was meant by keeping it flat.

The art of the piano passed him by before he was sixty. But his *Gradus* remains permanently in use, while his "instructive" sonatas have

declined chiefly into those villages and provincial towns where teachers yet continue to
make the work of pupils dull, dry, or hopelessly
wearisome. To play the *Gradus* is to become
exhilarated ; to play the sonatas at any length
is to wonder why music exists ; yet it is well to
know of the sonata named *Didone Abbandonata*.

XV. DUSSEK

Working in the same generation as Clementi, but as different from him as love is from liking, is the pianist Johann Ludwig Dussek, born nine years after Clementi and nine years before Beethoven, in the Bohemian town of Tschaslau, or, as the name stands in Bohemian, Czaslaw.

He was a warm-blooded and emotional man, and his nature comes out in his music. Clementi was of that genial temperament which readily becomes jovial ; he was of a thoroughly " engaging " deportment ; but he had the calculating eye, and he was too sanely successful in life, and in all the little by-paths of life, to give us the pleasure that Dussek gives us.

Dussek lived a long time in London, and he and the great Italian were friends. It was a habit of the virtuosos to go into business, and Dussek was for a time a business man ; but while Clementi made money, retiring with a big fortune into Worcestershire, Dussek lost money, and as the money was not his own, but his creditors', he had to run away.

Except to the great-great-grandheirs of his creditors, Dussek lives pleasantly in history— it is as grateful to think of him as it is enjoyable to look at his portrait.

Music teemed within him almost as abundantly as in Schubert, though more coarsely and to far less vital purpose. The masters are not prodigals, but economists, able to take a simple idea and work it into a grand, organic form.

DUSSEK

Men of the third rank, like Dussek, are dominated by their fancy and invention, not rulers and controllers of the same.

It is not enough in art to have ideas—or, as young people generally phrase it, to have imagination. You must have in addition the power to command the working of that imagination, the skill to make its products clear and concise, and the high courage for hard work.

§

His father, an organist, taught him to play the piano at four, the organ at eight, and to sing as soon as his voice showed itself. Leaving home in 1777, at the age of sixteen, young Ladislaw did not return for twenty-five years, nor did he see his father again until that period had passed by. He went first to Prague University, where he took a degree in some branch of philosophy, and then wandered off upon the career of a virtuoso pianist.

Before long he met with a Count Männer, who became his patron in the manner of the eighteenth century. This nobleman took him into Holland, where Dussek up to 1782 worked as organist and teacher. His last church post was at Berg-op-Zoom—a dull place for such a man. From here he removed to Amsterdam.

He was already known as a musician of excellent attainment as well as one of still finer

163

promise. His fame spread widely from Amsterdam ; the future appeared very secure : but so anxious was he not to misapply his musical abilities that after a year or two he went to Hamburg to ask advice of Philipp Emanuel Bach, then nearly at the end of his life, and now experiencing the benefit of that long effort to acquire the calm strength of a living philosophy.

Bach advised him to follow his art of the pianoforte : he told him that his gifts were unusual, but begged him to study himself closely, and always to aim for the truest and highest kind of music.

The young Bohemian wanted to obey these recommendations. But there was an easy cleverness in his nature that inclined him to enter paths leading to immediate success. Moreover, the average interest of the public was no purer then than now ; and while a severe art was unprofitable, showmanship and novelty paid all along the line.

And so when in 1784 Dussek entered on a long tour in Germany and other countries, he entertained the people with performances on the harmonica as well as on the piano.

II

The harmonica is the instrument generally referred to in English literature as the musical

DUSSEK

glasses.* It consisted of glass basins partly immersed in water, which were made to revolve, and which, on being touched by the fingers, gave forth musical notes. All the glasses revolved at the same time ; each gave its own note ; and a chord could be sounded of as many notes as the performer could touch glasses.

Playing was an exciting occupation. The sounds were peculiarly emotional, the tone having a penetrating quality, and the nerves of the performer were affected in a curious way.

There were virtuosos of the instrument— Marianne Davies, Marianna Kirchgessner (who was blind), Naumann, our Dussek, and several others, as the Princess Louise, Grand Duchess of Darmstadt, C. F. Pohl (the father), and the Leipzig musician, J. C. Müller. The latter wrote a Method of Playing the Harmonica. Naumann composed whole sonatas for the instrument. Mozart provided one or two pieces for Marianna Kirchgessner, and Beethoven threw off a little piece for one of his friends.

Thus Dussek had some authority for adopting the harmonica ; he was not as Steibelt with his tambourine and triangle ; yet he fell here from the standard recommended by Bach, and for the time being is almost a showman.

---

*" (The ladies) would talk of nothing but high life ... pictures, taste, Shakespear, and the musical glasses."—*The Vicar of Wakefield*, 1761.

" Some men are like musical glasses—to produce their finest tones you must keep them wet."—COLERIDGE, *Table-Talk*, 1834.

MAKERS OF MUSIC

III

This wandering life lasted up to 1790. Dussek found a friend in a Prince Radziwell, with whom he lived for a year in Lithuania. In France he found another friend in Marie Antoinette. He was not particularly comfortable in Italy, because the Italians, never fond of the piano, wanted more of his harmonica than he cared to offer.

The Revolution drove him to London in 1790. Here at once he became a popular pianist and a fashionable teacher. The musicians respected him. Haydn, in London for the Salomon concerts of 1792, wrote to the father Dussek (far away in Czaslaw) to say what an eminent professor of music his son had become, and how upright and moral he was as a man. " I love him just as you do," says Haydn, " for he fully deserves my love."

Dussek fell in love with the daughter of Domenico Corri, a London composer and publisher. He and the girl married in 1792, and Dussek went into partnership with his father-in-law. Business was good, and they would have made money. But the junior partner neglected his duties after a while ; things went wrong, and in 1800 he had to leave the country, since otherwise he would have been put into the prison for debtors.

The ten years spent in London were the longest period of stationary life he was to know. The spirit of wandering had been around him for some time, and he was not sorry of this excuse to go back to Europe.

From Hamburg—a place for which he had always a warm affection—Johann Ludwig gradually made his way home to Bohemia ; and there, in the year 1802, he and his family were together again, after the long separation of twenty-five years.

He was now middle-aged, being forty-one, with only another ten years of life remaining to him ; but of those ten years there were three that were to form the most important part of his life, namely, his association with Prince Louis Ferdinand of Prussia.

IV

Prince Louis, nephew of Frederick the Great, was a good, solid musician, by far the most gifted in our art of all the members of his family. He was a great pianist, surpassed only by men like Dussek. Beethoven thought highly of his playing when they met in 1796, and still more highly of his musicianship when they met again in 1804. The prince wrote a considerable amount of chamber music, the larger part of which is published.

He was a soldier, and wherever he was— whether stationed in a garrison, or in camp— he carried his musical establishment with him and filled the evenings with music.

MAKERS OF MUSIC

The programmes were planned and rehearsed in the early morning. During the military manœuvres in the summer of 1805, which took place near Magdeburg (Dussek was with the prince from 1803 to 1806), Spohr, the young violinist, was a member of the establishment. He tells us that he and Dussek would be summoned at six in the morning, or even earlier, to attend the prince in his reception room. As the summons was imperative, there would be no time to dress, and they had to hurry along in dressing-gown and slippers. They would find the prince at the piano, clad only in shirt, drawers, and stockings ; and rehearsal would begin at once. Their spirits would be high. Rehearsal would go on until everything was satisfactory. Often it ran into the hours fixed for the prince's reception of his staff and the issuing and receiving of military orders for the day. And so in the room would be officers in full field uniform, and musicians in dressing-gowns.

A good deal of time was spent in Berlin during these three years. The three great pianists there were Dussek, Prince Louis Ferdinand, and Friedrich Heinrich Himmel (1765-1814), and much piano music was made throughout the place. Berlin musicians used to say fifty years later that the influence of those three years was still to be felt in their town, especially that which emanated from Dussek.

DUSSEK

The prince preferred the English piano to the Viennese, because the touch was firmer and the tone more rich. There were qualities of energy and splendour in his musicianship, and he was in every way brilliantly alive. Much wine was drunk.

Prince Louis is the man to whom Beethoven dedicated his pianoforte concerto in C minor, Op. 37 ; composed 1800, published 1804. In the latter year Louis Ferdinand was visiting Prince Lobkowitz of Bohemia, who had recently bought Beethoven's new symphony in E flat— the *Eroica*. On the day preceding Prince Louis' departure, the symphony was played at the evening music-making. It so pleased Louis that he asked for it to be at once repeated ; and then, when supper was over, asked for it a third time, since he was to depart the next day and might not have another opportunity to hear the music for a long while.*

On October 10th, 1806, in a battle between the French and the Prussians, Prince Louis was killed. He was thirty-four. Dussek commemorated the death of his friend by means of one of his finest compositions—the *Elégie*

---

*A story is told of a countess who gave a dinner in honour of the prince, with music before and after, Beethoven among the musicians. She insulted Beethoven by not offering him a place at the table, although the prince's regard for him was well-known. Beethoven, in a rage, left the house. A day or two later the prince in his turn gave a dinner, to which he invited the countess and the composer, placing them at the head of the table with him, one on either hand. Beethoven was pleased with this mark of distinction and in later years often spoke of it.

harmonique sur la mort de Louis Ferdinand, Prince de Prusse (Op. 61). He likewise wrote a " consolation " (Op. 62), which was very popular while people were sentimentally regretting the death of the prince.

V

After spending a year in the service of the Prince of Isenburg, Dussek removed to Paris, where he passed the last four years of his life in the service of Prince Talleyrand. The cause of his death was gout, which crept up to his brain. With him when he died was Sigismund Neukomm, the pianist, who afterwards became pianist to Prince Talleyrand.

Those four years in Paris brought Dussek to the height of his fame, and his death was deeply regretted by musicians all over Europe. There were many famous performers in the city when he arrived—Lamare the 'cellist, Baillot and Rode the violinists, Steibelt and Woelfl the pianists ; but Dussek seems to have been the most liked of all.

Until we begin to read carefully about this man, we have the impression that he was gay, wild, and, indeed, dissipated. But he was not this. He had the liberal mind, with no talent for jealousy ; he was kind, very sympathetic, and honourable (for all that he ran from his London reditors). His moral faults were those of a high-

DUSSEK

spirited and emotional man, who had **to live in** the liveliest artistic and social world.

He wrote a good deal of music—53 piano sonatas ; 9 piano sonatas for two players ; 80 violin sonatas ; 12 piano concertos ; 10 piano trios ; and a mass of miscellaneous works. His earlier experiences on the organ made his music unlike that of other pianists of the time— it is full-toned, melodious (in the manner of his playing), noble in a pleasant way, and curiously fluent. His art is quite other than the art of Clementi, for here are imagination and real feeling, of recognizable character and per- sonality. Some of his slow movements have a grave sweetness and an unquestionable sincerity,

with a general fullness that, being integral in the idea, reminds you of the great masters. If his technique were modern, and if his construction were more intellectual, we should say Dussek was a " romantic."

His mission in music was a contemporary one. While Clementi was perfecting a clear technique, and while the virtuosos, with their " glitter and splash," were opening the way for Chopin and Liszt, Dussek made the piano an instrument for true music ; and while the great music of Beethoven was awaiting the time when a general understanding of it should enable it to spread through the world, Dussek's music prepared a path for it by teaching people to appreciate the new German music in looser and more easily assimilable forms. He extended the school of Philipp Emanuel Bach ; and it was actually said by critics in the generation after his death that he had done more for German music than even the great masters of his time (Haydn, Mozart, and Beethoven).

His piano music died slowly, and even now it is not wholly dead. There will never be a revival of these works, because a later generation never recovers the forgotten or discarded art of an earlier time, except when that art is of pure form ; but the advanced student of piano playing should know something of at least the three sonatas included in the Peters Edition, No. 274— Op. 10, in G minor ; Op. 70, in A flat (*Le*

retour à Paris) ; and Op. 77, in F minor
(*L'invocation*). With all their faults, these pieces
contain the supreme virtue of perfect phrasing ;
their clauses are clear as the lines of a poem,
and they teach us how to deliver music in phrase
and proportion, which is what Beethoven demanded, and which Liszt, in his reform of the
art of conducting, strove to convey to his
orchestra by his gestures. That is to say, Dussek's
music helps us to perform music in the modern
way, which is the way of Rhythmical Declamation.

XVI.   THE MERCHANTS OF MUSIC

In the days of Beethoven, and on into the time of Chopin and Liszt, there were two groups of pianists—the teachers and the concert virtuosos.

The virtuosos were of two classes, the one meritorious and praiseworthy, the other detestable, being purveyors of the poorest music that has ever been given to the world of amateurs. This music was, of course, as good as its market deserved ; but the fact does not make the mongers less artistically despicable.

These men were very much in the fashion as performers, composers, and teachers. They had standing contracts with publishers in England, Germany, and France, to supply pieces to approved pattern, so many pieces per annum. The market price was good, ranging from £20 to £75 for a rondo, set of variations, fantasia, or sonata. It would take a man three or four days to knock together a sonata ; a rondo he could write at a sitting.

Schubert, of course, could write several songs at a sitting ; but his best rate of payment from the publishers was about a shilling a song.

The great virtue of this music was that it was easy to play, but sounded hard. It was, moreover, reminiscent. Its technicalities were those of the exercises and études. Its themes were popular songs or familiar operatic airs. The patterns were simple, descending frequently to the form of a set of quadrilles. A few of the pieces are still in use, as, for example, Th. Oesten's *The Mermaid's Song from Oberon*, which can be bought in Penny Bazaars, the village shops where they sell tobacco and music, and similar places. And in country districts unhappy pupils still work at pieces that have on the title-page names like Karr, Hünten, Asher, Rivona, Ch. Voss, F. Beyer, Burgmüller, Henri Cramer, and Henri Rosellen, which by accident have survived.

The amateur pianists used to have their music bound up together in a heavy volume. They learned so many pieces in the course of their studies, and whatever they learned they pre-served in the volume—even the sheets of technical exercises. Occasionally as the years went by they bought and learned other pieces ; and when these had accumulated, they had them bound into a second volume. Music of all kinds went within the same covers, from sonatas to part-songs.

Thousands of these volumes remain in England to-day. They can be bought for a shilling or two at old book-shops. To look through one is to be shown, more vividly than by any other possible means, the low level of art maintained by the fashionable teachers and performers of the time. . . . There was a Miss M. Coleman, who about the year 1817 had her second set of pieces bound into a volume. The opening numbers are as follows :

MAKERS OF MUSIC

1. "God Save the King," arranged for the Pianoforte with New Variations and an Introductory Movement and Coda, Composed and Respectfully Inscribed to Miss Louisa Sheldon, by William Dance, Musician in Ordinary to His Majesty. The Third Edition. Pub'd Aug't 1809.

The Introduction is made of scraps of Handelian music, remembered sub-consciously by Mr. Dance, and carried on as long as the habit of music suggests, until the music settles into recollections of Clementi The tune is given out with each phrase repeated. The variations, which are four in number, are meaningless technical exercises.

2. "Introduction et Air Caledonien, varié pour le Piano Forte, avec Accompagnement de Flute, ad Libitum; par G. Kiallmark.

The Caledonian Air is ' Ye Banks and Braes." The remark " *ad libitum* " means that it does not matter whether the flute part is played or not. One of the variations presents the song in the form of a jerky mar h.

3. Theme Allemand, with Variations for the Piano Forte, composed by F. Kalkbrenner.
4. "Huntsman Rest." With Variations for the Piano Forte with an Accompaniment

for the Flute. Composed and Inscribed to The Right Honourable Lady Georgina Moly-neux, by J. Mazzinghi.

5. " The Plough Boy " as a Rondo by Dussek.

6. " O dear, what can the matter be ? " A Favourite Air with Variations for the Piano Forte, composed by F. Latour.

7. " Le Retour de Windsor." A New Sonata for the Piano Forte, With or Without the Additional Keys. With an Accompaniment for a Violin (ad Libitum). Composed and Dedicated to Miss Olympia Cazalet by Mr. Latour. Op. 9.

The second movement is a rondo on the tune " Windsor Park." On the title page is an engraving of Windsor Castle.

All the pianists, from Dussek to Moscheles, provided these fashionable pieces; and Beethoven merely demonstrated what good might come of the habit when he wrote his variations on *God Save the King* and *Rule Britannia.*

XVII. STEIBELT TO CZERNY

DANIEL STEIBELT (1765-1823) used to sell the same set of pieces to two publishing firms, generally with one of the *ad libitum* flute or violin parts added to the copy supplied to one of the publishers. A year at least would elapse before the fraud was discovered. Each publisher would make profitable sales in his particular country; and no one seems to have minded much, for Steibelt could always sell his goods.

He was a wanderer, like Dussek, but was in every other way different from that musician, being arrogant, jealous, and insufferably rude. His rudeness and pride were born of extreme vanity, which turned the musicians against him immediately, and which made him unwelcome even to the fashionable amateurs after a year or two.

A fashionable public enjoys contact with what is called the Artistic Temperament, and is thrilled by the bad manners that are supposed to indicate possession of the Artistic Temperament; but this toy, as all others, is changed often, and it does not profit an artist.

Steibelt was a brilliant player, but his sense of quiet beauty in music was defective, and he did not play slow passages well. The Germans thought little of him, and his fame lay chiefly in Paris, London, and Petersburg. In 1798 he married a girl who played the tambourine, and henceforth she used to accompany him at the piano with that instrument.

One of the many contests of the time took place between this man and Beethoven. He had been very rude to Beethoven just before the event, and this brought Beethoven to that rage in which he always played best. After Steibelt had performed his improvisation on a theme by Beethoven, Beethoven improvised on a theme of Steibelt's in such a fiery, impassioned manner that his opponent ran from the room, and would never again remain in his company.

Sometimes these contests were pleasant, filled with fun and frolic, and rising in the end to high-spirited gaming between the competitors. Those between Beethoven and Woelfl were of that happy kind.

II

This Joseph Woelfl (1772-1812) was one of the finer virtuosos. His hands were so large that he could play tenths where the normal pianists can play only octaves ; that is, he could play scales in double tenths, also arpeggios in tenths. This wide stretch, and the power corresponding, gave him a unique command of contrapuntal music, which he turned to the advantage of his extemporizing, until in this department of piano art he was one of the leaders. His style of playing was broad and large, and enormously energetic.

He and Beethoven had a mutual respect. Beethoven was rough, as we know, and nothing made his roughness apparent so completely as the arrogance of a Steibelt ; Woelfl was witty and courteous and pleasant—he refused to be put out by Beethoven's manner, and the end of it was that these two were often very jolly together.

Woelfl was no showman. He wrote plenty of rubbish for the amateur market ; but he knew it was rubbish, and in his more personal music tried to be worthy his art. This pianist's fame was at its height in Paris from 1801 to 1805. In the latter year he came to London, where he died at the age of forty.

III

Kalkbrenner, christened Friedrich Wilhelm Michael (1784-1849), one of the adored teacher-virtuosos of those days, was as vain as Steibelt, though not palpably arrogant. He was an earnest money-maker, who never said a cross word to a critic. In many respects, he took music to a lower point than it reached in the hands of any of his contemporaries.

He was quiet and self-possessed, with that equable manner that comes of a good account in the bank and of a secure teaching connection. Such a man offends no one openly : in 1823 Mendelssohn's sister Fanny said that Kalkbrenner was " an accomplished, amiable gentleman, and

to blame or praise more agreeably than he does
is not possible." But in 1832, when Mendelssohn,
now famous, was in Paris, Kalkbrenner was very
jealous of him—" ready to eat me from envy,"
Mendelssohn said.

> He is the only musician here who acts
> unkindly and hypocritically towards me ; and
> though I never placed much confidence in
> him, still it is always a very painful sensation
> to know that you are in the society of a person
> who hates you, but is careful not to show it.

A little later Mendelssohn was in London,
where he met the Moscheles family again. Of
these (having Kalkbrenner in mind) he wrote :

> They are excellent people, and after so long
> an interval, it is most cheering once more to
> meet an artist who is not a victim to envy,
> jealousy, or miserable egotism.

As to Kalkbrenner's playing, of which many
accounts have come down to us, that of young
Charles Hallé gives as clear a picture as any :

> In Kalkbrenner's playing there reigns a
> clearness, a distinctness, and neatness that
> are astonishing ; in octave scales he has an
> immense facility and precision, especially in
> the left hand ; then he has a special mode of

handling the piano, particularly in melodious passages, which makes a great impression, but which I cannot describe to you ; the reason of it lies merely in that he keeps his fingers so closely over the keys.

Most young people admired Kalkbrenner, and it was actually an idea of Chopin's, when he first went to Paris, that he should take lessons from him. Mendelssohn, however, told Chopin that he could not do him any good ; and when Hallé, some six weeks after the writing of the letter just quoted from, heard Chopin play, he said, " Kalkbrenner, compared with Chopin, is a child."

IV

Chopin was influenced by two musicians— John Field and Hummel. Field was the most famous of the pupils of Clementi ; Hummel, one of the greatest of the Viennese pianists, derived some of the essentials of his art from Mozart : thus Clementi and Mozart meet in Chopin.

Liszt was influenced by Beethoven and Chopin, and taught by Czerny, the greatest of all the Viennese teachers. From Liszt flows the main stream of modern piano playing.

A short account of Field, Hummel, and Czerny will, therefore, serve to close the present

FIELD

collective chapter ; after which an account of
Moscheles, the last of the pianists before Chopin
and Liszt, will fittingly conclude this sketch of
the earlier stages of the art of clavier and piano
playing.

▼

The early history of John Field shows several
persons in a poor light, among them his master
Clementi.

The boy's father and grandfather, respectively
a violinist and an organist, seeing that he was
gifted, put him to music. This was good ; but
they kept him so unmercifully close to his
practising that he was always miserable and
would have run away, had there been a place to
run to.

Eventually he was apprenticed to Clementi.
The father had to pay Clementi a hundred guineas
fee, which proves that he was anxious to do the
right thing by his son. The great teacher taught
John Field well, which again was good ; but
he also made excessive use of him in his musical
warehouse, where it was the youth's duty to
show pianos to prospective customers. Nearly
all the virtuosos of this period were engaged in
business, either as instrument makers or as music
publishers ; and it was almost an established
custom to make this convenience of their pupils.
Clementi, however, was rather cruel to Field :

the young musician was shy, awkward, and sensitive, rarely comfortable with strangers, and therefore painfully conscious of his appearance ; yet his master did not look after his clothes ; and as the boy grew rapidly, what he wore was always too small for him. He was very unhappy here. Again he would have run away, but could see no opening in the world for such a melancholy self-deprecating individual.

Field was twenty in the year 1802, when his master took him on a Continental concert tour. In Paris he at once astonished the people by his playing of Bach, Handel, and other masters. He had that beautiful touch which produces the singing tone of the piano. Into that tone he brought an infinitude of gradations, so that the piano seemed almost as a violin. His music was smooth, equal, and strangely quiet.

When they reached Petersburg, where Clementi had a piano warehouse, Field had again to act as display-salesman. Now, however, he had grown to manhood. He also saw that he could make a living for himself. Therefore when Clementi left Russia, Field stayed behind, glad at last to be relieved of his servitude.

For twenty years he lived in Petersburg and Moscow, a favourite performer and fashionable teacher. Then he went on a concert tour, which ended disastrously in Italy. The Italians did not care for his art ; and as he had for some years been an intemperate man, spending in a moment

what he earned, he at once became destitute.
Illness came upon him, and it seemed that he
was doomed to die among strangers. This was
in 1835, when Field was fifty-three.

However, a family of Russians discovered
him. With these he went back to Moscow,
staying for a little while in Vienna, where his
playing of his nocturnes charmed the public.
But his health was permanently broken, and
two years later he died.

It is by his nocturnes that we know him to-day.
These—the model for Chopin—set a pianoforte
style that has remained with every composer,
whatever his nature and whatever the form in
which he writes. Liszt, who thought highly of
Field, said of him that " he was the first to introduce a style deriving its origin from none of the
existing forms ; in which feeling and melody
exclusively prevailed, liberated from the fetters
and dross of an enforced form. He cleared the
way for all subsequent efforts appearing under
the names of *Songs without Words*, *Impromptus*,
Ballades, and the like ; and up to him can be
traced the origin of those pieces which are designed
to express, through tone, particular phases of
emotion and warm feeling."

Spohr, who met Clementi and Field, said
that the master was bright, jovial, and active,
and the pupil pale, tall, thin, and dreamily
melancholy, but altogether romantic-looking.

MAKERS OF MUSIC

As John Field was a pupil of Clementi's, so Hummel was a pupil of Mozart's, in whose house he lived for two years, receiving few regular lessons, but hearing him play continually. He was nine when the two years were over. A concert tour, in company with his father, brought him to London, where for another two years he studied under Clementi.

Hummel was of the earlier Viennese school of pianists. He preferred a dry tone, with little use of the pedal. His precision was remarkable ; but it was the precision of a photograph, with none of the richness, warmth, and softened outlines of an imaginative picture. His main course of development was in the treatment of the treble register of the piano, which by men like Steibelt was played only in a bright and flashy way.

When, in 1829, Hummel made his last tour, his age being fifty-one years, he found that his art was now old-fashioned. The English still liked him, but the French, enraptured by Kalkbrenner, did not want him.

Among his pupils were Czerny, Thalberg, Hiller, and Henselt. He was an earnest theoretician of the science of piano playing, but his great Method proved too complex ; and, moreover, it could not compete with the miraculously practical Methods of Czerny.

HUMMEL

Hummel was a large, clumsy man, who dressed for comfort, not looks, and whose face is as unlike a musician's as can well be imagined He died in 1837, the year of his birth being 1778.

He was a composer in the large forms, and his Masses are still sung occasionally

vii

Carl Czerny (1791-1857) succeeded above all other teachers, because he observed and analysed the fingers and minds of his pupils in the way the teacher of singing works to produce a voice correctly.

In the whirling, stormy, kaleidoscopic period of the virtuosos, when some dozens of men were ceaselessly travelling Europe, playing here one week and there the next, rarely living a year in one place, and not always actuated by the noblest of ideals, Czerny was as a peaceful light burning steadily in one locality. His life, quieter by far even than Tartini's, was spent in his native town ; for only three times did he travel abroad, and his first journey was not taken until he was forty-four.

He was a modest man, simple and unassuming: He never married, and had no brothers or sisters. Until his parents died he lived with them ; and the peace of this home so moved Beethoven, who never had a home at all in the true sense of the word, that he asked to be allowed to live there—it was arranged that he should do this, but one of the old folk fell ill, and the proposal came to nothing. There would, of course, have been no more peace at the Czernys' if Beethoven had gone there.

Carl Czerny gave up playing in public early in life. Moreover, he withdrew from social engagements, so as to be free for his art. Yet he was a famous teacher, and in Vienna famous teachers were almost expected to mingle freely at parties given in the houses of their pupils.

This man was of a sensitive disposition. Vulgarity or coarseness, even when attended by wit, caused him to shrink in pain ; and contact with any of the baser passions, as jealousy and greed, gave him distress of soul.

His masters were Beethoven, Hummel, and Clementi. Beethoven he loved ; and Beethoven had for him that fatherly affection which was so strong in his mighty character. Czerny knew Hummel after he had finished studying with Beethoven, and he tells us that Hummel's playing was a revelation to him of what could be done in the matter of speed, clarity, and certainty.

He started to teach at the age of thirteen, continuing for more than forty years. He aimed to teach the production of an external luxuriousness—a quality which is very charming, and which the pianola of to-day can readily create. And so the essentials of his method were brightness, pearliness of tone, and almost perpetual brilliance. He did not go into the emotional depths of music or strive after high passion. We can, indeed, say that he was concerned with the performer, not the music performed ; and with this we may be satisfied, for a man like Czerny was needed at that moment in the art of piano playing as imperatively as a man like Beethoven was needed in the art of writing sonatas and symphonies. He was the right man in the right moment, but for whom there might have been no Liszt for another generation.

Czerny was so complete a master of technicalities, and so wise and experienced a teacher, that in the midst of a lesson he could write the exercise or study a pupil suddenly showed himself to be in need of.

He taught only students of exceptional promise, yet even then he had to give from ten to twelve lessons a day. On Sunday evenings he used to give concerts, at which his more advanced pupils played. Beethoven used to come to these meetings.

Czerny wrote thousands of pieces, from short piano studies to Masses and symphonies. No single example of his serious music is performed to-day, nor will any of it ever be heard again. His arrangements of orchestral works, however, are often played ; though not, I imagine, that arrangement for sixteen players on eight pianos of the *William Tell* overture, made at the request of a publisher. His studies are in constant use.

189

MAKERS OF MUSIC

The 101 *Exercises* are the first cause of distress to the pupils of ordinary teachers, and his larger books of studies are probably worked at by every advanced student in the entire world.

Of the pianists gathered into this chapter Kalkbrenner and Steibelt are to be least admired. Woelfl and Hummel are to be respected. Field is to be regarded as a genius in the matter of the nocturnes. But Czerny, I believe, is to be looked on as a friend.

XVIII.   MOSCHELES

With Moscheles we come into contact with a
musician who, himself dual-natured, lived in
the period of transition from the old to the new
in piano playing. Born twenty-five years later,
he would have been among the romantic composers
and the Liszt players. As it was, the music he
wrote hovered from the fashionable to the serious,
and his manner of performance remained of the
general school of Clementi, Hummel, Czerny,
and the others who filled the end of the eighteenth
century and the beginning of the nineteenth.

His life was lengthy. It extended into the
year 1870, occupied to the last with teaching.
He therefore worked in his grove nearly a generation after the new manner of playing had been
perfected, and among his pupils were musicians
who are still alive and who have told us how
different their master was from the " modernists "
of the middle of the century.

Fate so planned the life, character, and circumstances of this musician that within fifty
years of his death he should be but a name, with
scarcely anything of his work exerting a traceable
influence. Yet it is good, and perhaps necessary,
to know of him, because not only does he sum up
the first great period of piano playing, but by
contrast he enables us to understand the nature
of the second great period, which is ours.

MAKERS OF MUSIC

I

The father of Ignaz Moscheles (1794-1870), a cloth merchant of Prague, being an amateur musician who played the guitar and sang, was determined that one of his children should be a " thoroughbred " performer. Out of the five, he selected the eldest daughter, engaging as teacher an old local professor named Zadrahka, who by this engagement, and by this alone, has had his name retained in a by-path of history, all else relative to him, as of thousands of similar workers, being forgotten.

The year would be about 1798. The father's selection proved bad. Little Miss Moscheles had clumsy fingers. Her mind was slow. She stumbled through her lessons, and in the intervals between them she practised dutifully—but all without happiness. Not that old Zadrahka minded. He was used to dull pupils ; and eighteenpence, the price of a lesson, was eighteenpence, whether earned amid brilliance or not.

But Ignaz, a child about four years old, minded very much. He was a natural musician. When the weather was fine, he was always out in front of the guard-house to watch the band play their music while the guard was changing— he was even one of the boys who were picked by the bandsmen to hold the music on a windy day, and proud to be thus employed in the service of

Art. Already, in fact, he had determined to be a *spielmann* when he grew up.

From the beginning Ignaz had attended his sister's lessons, standing close against the little pianoforte and taking in Zadrahka's remarks. When the instrument was not in use, he had exercised his fingers in the approved manner and had committed to memory the sounds of his sister's little pieces ; finding, therefore, no particular difficulty in doing by himself what Zadrahka wanted, he observed her clumsiness with scorn and impatience.

And so one day when the girl was more clumsy than usual, and even old Zadrahka looked at the clock, Ignaz said, in the proper spirit of family life :

" Dear me, how stupid ! I could do that better myself."

Teacher and pupil welcomed the interruption. Ignaz demanded permission to show what he could do. The old man lifted him on to the stool, and the child proved that he could indeed do as he said.

Zadrahka reported the matter to the father. When the next lesson-day arrived, the girl was told she could give up her music if she wished to, and Ignaz was told he might take her place.

But now Zadrahka was not altogether happy. He found his new pupil had ideas, while he himself had only a method. The boy wanted to know " Why " and " Wherefore," which in-

MAKERS OF MUSIC

formation such an instructor is not accustomed to give. Worse still, Ignaz learned so fast that quite soon he knew all the old man was used to put before his pupils. What occupied a year was now compressed into less than a month. Furthermore, this boy had a musical curiosity. He wanted to have endless compositions played to him ; and spending his pocket-money at a Circulating Library, he brought pieces to the lesson, asking Zadrahka first to play these, and secondly to give him lessons on them. The pieces were by the admired masters Eberl, Kozeluch, and the like, with whom Zadrahka had not much acquaintance.

Before long, therefore, the old man retired, losing one pupil of his round, but gaining a peace of mind of greater value than the lost two thalers. Such a pupil as Ignaz was as disturbing to him as a "new" composer in an age of musical conservatism.

II

The cloth merchant was a wise parent. He was loving and gentle (as was his son all through his later life, and also his son's wife, these two filling the records of their time with friendliness, consideration, and quiet, earnest thought for others). The father was anxious that Ignaz should cultivate his talent modestly and sanely. He tried to put a stop to the admiring ejaculations of female relatives, which he thought must for certain unsettle the child. He also tried to keep Ignaz to steady practising ; for the child rather disliked his scales and exercises, preferring a frequent change of pieces at the Subscription Library. Ignaz, moreover, was captain and costumier of an important troupe of soldiers, brigands, and French Revolutionaries ; and his time was seriously required for the making of wooden swords, pasteboard helmets, and the like responsibilities.

The new teacher, a man named Horzelsky, was dangerously modernistic, for by the time Ignaz was seven he was teaching him the *Sonata pathétique* of that overbold musician, Beethoven. This was bad for the child, mentally and technically ; and at last the cloth merchant took his son to Dionys Weber, the leading musician of Prague, to ask his advice what to do with him.

Ignaz, dressed by his mother in his best clothes, played the Beethoven sonata, this being his best piece. He was much put out at the close not to hear any bravos or other exclamations of wondering delight from the gentleman sitting in the room ; and he only half understood what was meant when the gentleman said :

" The boy is on the wrong road. He has talent, and I can make something of him if you will place him unreservedly in my hands for three years. The first year he will play Mozart, the second Clementi, and the third Bach. There will be no Beethoven until, by the aid of these three masters, he may have become equal to the task of playing Beethoven's music. If he once goes to the Subscription Libraries, I have done with him."

The cloth merchant, agreeing to these stipulations, undertook to place his son with Weber. On the way home, he explained things to Ignaz, saying how if he worked well he would bring credit on himself and on the family.

Ignaz did not like giving up the Subscription Library. As is the case with all active musicians in the first stage of their experience of playing, he was interested in all kinds of music—the good because it moved some vague faculty in him, issuing a challenge no less delightful to accept because not fully understood, and the bad because it excited him. Such a musician will at this time work for an hour at a Bach fugue, and then turn with an almost impassioned pleasure to a set of quadrilles, a march, a battle-piece, or an idyll expressing home-sickness.

But of course he consented, and for the three years worked under Dionys Weber. His father generally came for him after the lesson, and if the professor's report was good, the two used to call at a confectioner's on the way home.

After a while, the reward took the form of seats at the Opera. Here was a great reward indeed. The music seized hold of the boy, and when they reached home he would at once go to the piano and play over the marches, dances, and airs that had moved his imagination and fixed themselves in his memory. By the piano would sit the cloth merchant, proud of his son's ability, and every now and then remarking how impatiently he was waiting to hear Ignaz's first composition.

In his fourteenth year the boy was well advanced in theory of music, and he was busy writing a piece on a melody used in the Synagogue with which to make his first appearance in public. But the father was not to hear this. He was suddenly taken ill with typhus, and died, leaving the family none too well off.

The mother was anxious to know what to do with Ignaz. In the family was an old uncle who recommended business, prophesying ruin and a wasted life if music was allowed to occupy the boy's time. The best he could hope for, he said, would be to play the fiddle in a beer-garden. But Dionys Weber said, keep to music, be steady, and you will make good. The boy played his concerto at a concert in the town. The success was encouraging enough ; and a year or so later she allowed Ignaz to leave home for Vienna ; alone, and—of necessity—dependent entirely upon himself.

III

Ignaz was soon accepted by the musicians and music lovers of Vienna. Evening parties, at which music formed the chief entertainment, took place all the year round. These were useful to young professional singers, teachers, and violinists ; for though when invited as guests they played and sang without fee, the parties served to introduce them to the principal lesson receiving public of the city. Indeed, a musician setting out to establish himself in such a place as Vienna was mainly concerned, in the beginning, to secure introductions in the fashionable world that would lead to invitations to these parties. Ignaz Moscheles came with good recommendations from Prague ; he was a pleasant youth, of charming artistic attainments ; and within a short while he had a number of pupils and as many social engagements as he could find time to attend.

Observing the Viennese manner of piano playing, which was based on a light, swift finger action, he adapted it to his own style.

One of the delights of the Viennese in the matter of piano playing was the sight of recognizable difficulties overcome and executed with absolute ease. However intricate or speedy the music, its rendering must be seemingly effortless. Consequently there must be nothing of extreme emotional or dramatic energy in the music or in the performer's conception of the music, because such an energy drew attention away from the chief element of the art that charmed the people, and was otherwise disturbing.

MOSCHELES

Our pianola, correctly played in light, swift music (as in a Mendelssohn *presto*), and unconditioned by the pianolist's personality, is as a great pianist of early Viennese school.

A year or two after his coming to Vienna, Moscheles met Meyerbeer, then a brilliant virtuoso of the instrument, and intending to live the life of a pianist ; he greatly admired his style : but he did not much admire Beethoven's style, because it lacked clearness and precision and was excessively impassioned. Moscheles, of course, admired Beethoven's music, now as always.

In 1808 he studied theory under Albrechtsberger, the authority on the art of composition who had taught Beethoven. He also studied under Salieri, the old Italian, who had not advanced in his liking for German music even to the works of Mozart. For three years Ignaz acted as assistant music master at the Royal Opera under Salieri, the pay for his services being chiefly a pass to all the performances.

Soon he was so busy teaching that he could refuse all pupils who did not show ability. His social engagements increased until every evening throughout the social season was occupied. His compositions found a market, so that he wrote largely. But he began work every morning at seven, practising the piano and the violin, and learning foreign languages—Italian, French, and English. " Those were happy and busy days in dear old Vienna ! " he said at the end of his life.

By 1814, when he was twenty years old, he had composed dozens of pieces. Their character can be gathered from a few titles—Descriptive Fantasia, *Triumphal Entry of the Allies into Paris* : Pianoforte Sonata, *The Return of the Kaiser* : Grand Duo Concertante for pianoforte and cello (or bassoon): *Rondo brillante* for four hands : a Cantata for the Jewish Congregations : variations, minuets, scherzos, rondos : and a sonata for violin and piano.

IV

In 1816 on the eve of his first concert tour, he went home for a while, giving some concerts in Prague. Dionys Weber and others who had believed in his musicianship were delighted with his advancement, because it proved them wise prophets. The old uncle apparently said nothing ; nor is anything reported of the old original master, Zadrahka—though Zadrahka by now was probably in a world where musicians do not have to go from family to family, giving lessons at eighteenpence a time.

In Vienna his fame as a pianist had developed so thoroughly that the amateurs of the town were divided into two camps, one acclaiming the velvet-like touch and pearly clarity of Hummel, the other the intellectual enthusiasm, youthful bravura, and swift energy of Moscheles. These two men, Hummel and Moscheles, were friends.

Ignaz was happy to be home again. He and his sisters amused themselves by imitating their childhood's games ; and he was proud to be able to ease his mother's anxiety over money matters.

His life in Vienna was now nearly over. The climax of his honours there had been a commission (in the year 1814) to make a pianoforte score of Beethoven's opera, *Fidelio*. This task brought him for a time into constant association with the great man. As the successive sections of the opera were finished, Moscheles used to go at once with the manuscript to Beethoven's house, where the master, if he was at home, at once read it, making very few alterations in the transcription. One morning Beethoven was still in bed when Moscheles arrived. He jumped up directly, and ran to the window in his shirt to look at the music. Some boys in the street began to dance and shout, staring at the window and pointing their fingers.

" What do those——boys want now ? " roared Beethoven.

Moscheles smiled, and pointed to Beethoven's shirt. Beethoven growled, but put on a dressing-gown.

When the score was finished, the arranger wrote on the last page, *The End, by the help of*

God. But the composer wrote under **the words,**
Oh Man ! *be thine own help.*

v

When twenty-two years old, Moscheles left
Vienna on his first concert tour. From 1816 to
1846 he worked as a concert virtuoso, teacher,
and composer, with his home fixed in London
for the last twenty-four years of the thirty.
From 1846 to 1870, the year of his death, he
lived in Leipzig, teaching at the Conservatorium
established by Mendelssohn.

The story of the last fifty-four years of his
life cannot be told here, because it would have
value only as it illustrated the general history of
music from before Berlioz to after Schumann.
Moscheles was a busy man, a leader of the second
order of the makers of music, chiefly in sympathy
with Mendelssohn of all living masters, and he
was left behind by Chopin and Liszt ; yet he
went everywhere, knew most of the people we
read of, and tried earnestly to understand music
as late as Wagner's *The Mastersingers ;* consequently his life could be made a view-point from
which one might survey European music up to
1870, and the student—when well informed of
the history of nineteenth-century music—would
do well to read carefully and constructively the
" Life of Moscheles " written by his wife, and
published in England in 1873.

MOSCHELES

VI

It was in the autumn of 1816 that Moscheles left Vienna, making his way to Leipzig in a slow and heavy vehicle, and passing the time as best he could with reading and practising on a little soundless clavier.

Musical conditions were pleasant in Leipzig. A delightful spirit of good fellowship and confidence prevailed. Everyone seemed to wish him well. At the rehearsal for his concert the bandsmen were helpful and obliging, and when he sat at the piano running through his solos they crowded round, admiring his delightful technique. But he was nervous, unable to eat all the day of the concert. At 6.30, the time of commencement, he swallowed a cup of tea, in which had been deposited a few drops of rum, gave the signal to start, and thereupon entered upon an evening which, as he said, he afterwards looked back on as one of the brightest and happiest of his life.

Matters were not so pleasant at Dresden. Social conditions were stiff there, and an official musician named Polledro, jealous of young Moscheles, put all kinds of hindrances in his way. However, the concert was a success.

Making his way through Holland andBelgium, he arrived at Paris. Here the people liked him. They were hospitable, and attended his concerts handsomely ; while Spohr, who was then in the city, and with whom Moscheles spent a good

203

deal of his spare time, was so little cared for by
the people that he had to cancel one concert,
owing to the small support promised

Life in Paris was very busy. A typical day is
the following : Practising and studying in the
early morning. After breakfast, an interview
with a Parisian musician brought in by a mutual
acquaintance, who wished to hear Moscheles
play in private and to discuss with him his
principles of piano technique Later in the
morning, a rehearsal with a violinist for the
evening engagement. At midday, attending
the performance of a Cherubini Mass at the
Court Chapel. In the early afternoon, attending
an orchestral rehearsal for a coming concert.
A long stroll afterwards with other musicians
who had been at the rehearsal, the walk accompanied by animated talk on musical subjects.
Further practising and studying at his rooms.
Dinner with friends at a restaurant. Finally, an
evening party at the private house of a duke or a
banker, where much music was offered, and
Moscheles played and extemporized. Home,
perhaps as late as four o'clock ; yet up again
the next day at seven

Moscheles made a good deal of money in
Paris, which made him happy, because he could
send still more and more to his mother in Prague.
From Paris he went to London, and so his life
continued up to 1823, when he returned for a
while to Vienna ; bearing with him—in addition

to the ordinary memories of a travelling musician,
who in a season sees a hundred famous people—
recollections of the high spirits and fun that
almost invariably fill the time of public musicians
in their free hours, and recollections further of
many law cases, it being a habit with him to
attend any trial (especially a murder trial) which
promised human interest.

VII

Friendship with the Mendelssohns began in
1824, when Moscheles gave Felix lessons in
piano playing. He saw at once that the boy of
fifteen was no prodigy, but already a master.
The next year he married a girl named Charlotte
Embden, of Hamburg, after a short acquaintance
only.

On the day of his marriage (which he called
his Day of Honour) he wrote in his diary,
" With the fullest sense of happiness, with
purity of heart and intention, and full of gratitude
to the Almighty, I entered this holy state, and
pray God to bless me." The marriage was very
happy; and his wife, a woman of ability, with a
delightful gift of observation, became as notable
as Moscheles for kindness to other musicians.

They settled in London, where they remained
until 1846. Moscheles played constantly, in
England and on the Continent, and he remained
one of the most popular musicians of his time,

as teacher, composer, concert-giver, pianist, and conductor. (He conducted the Birmingham Triennial Festival the year *Elijah* was produced.) But he never held any high official position, and the character of his private work can be gathered from the following advertisement :

Mr. Moscheles' Classes.

Mr. Moscheles, having of late been frequently applied to for Instruction in Harmony, Counterpoint, and Score-reading, begs to announce to his friends and the public that he means to open two classes at his own house; the first, for Amateur Ladies,* will be held on Monday mornings, from Eleven to One o'clock. In this Class, Mr. Moscheles purposes entering into the Science of Music so far as may enable ladies more fully to comprehend the construction of the compositions they hear, or wish to perform.

It is his intention, also, in the cases where nature has bestowed an inventive genius, to teach the correct notation of ideas. Instruction, too, will be given in reading the score, and accompanying. At the close of each lesson, Mr. Moscheles will perform some classical model piece, as an illustration of the best musical styles.

* That is, ladies who are musical amateurs, not amateurs in the state and condition of a gentlewoman.

MOSCHELES

The Second Class, to be held on Thursday Evenings, from five till seven, will be for young Professors, supposed to be somewhat prepared in Thorough Bass, who will be instructed in Practical Harmony, Fugue, and Counterpoint, as well as in the general rules of Composition. At these meetings, the writings of young composers may also be examined and revised.

Terms, Two Guineas per Month for each Pupil. The number of Pupils in each Class will be limited to Twenty.

December, 1843, No. 3, Chester Place, Regent's Park.

Assuming the class to fill, the teacher would receive ten guineas a lesson. This fact, which indicates the high value of Moscheles' position in London, must be borne in mind when considering his subsequent removal to Leipzig.

His style of playing, now as for twenty-five years preceding, was marked by " grace, elegance, and coquetry." He himself says, " I have always belonged to a school which aimed rather at clearness and accent than at loud hammering— at a correct understanding and truthful rendering of music than at surprising effects. It is my duty to show that one can play the piano without hammering; that such a thing as a pianissimo can be obtained without a soft pedal. The pedals are auxiliaries ; whoever makes them of primary importance puts in evidence the incapacity of his own fingers."

The new music of Chopin and Liszt, however, and the greater works of Beethoven, are not to be " correctly and truthfully rendered " in this style, because such compositions belong to another world than the world of Moscheles: they have " grace, elegance, and coquetry " at times, but at other times they have high dramatic intensity and a power of contrast which make the pedals not auxiliaries, but essentials.

Some of Liszt's art was objectionable to Moscheles, and though he worked constantly at Chopin, he could never really take to the music, because neither his ear nor his hand could encompass it. But he admired Chopin's playing, and thought differently of his music when he heard it performed by the composer.

VIII

Some years before 1846 Mendelssohn began to prepare for the establishing of a Conservatorium of Music at Leipzig. His chief concern was the teaching staff, and from the beginning he wanted Moscheles to be head of the piano playing department.

By the year 1846 the project had perfected itself, and it was necessary for Moscheles to make up his mind what to do. The problem was no small thing. He and his family belonged to London. For sixteen years they had lived in the house in Chester Place. Their permanent friends were there. His position was honourable and his income assured. Leipzig was a small town, with none of the artistic pleasures, and indeed few of the material comforts and conveniences, of London. But on the other hand life in London was hard; he was incessantly at work, and often there was a feverish activity around him. The calm of a life in the old German town spread itself gratefully before him; yet the salary of the principal teacher of piano playing in the new school was no more than a hundred and twenty pounds a year—a small sum, even though the post required only sixteen hours a week. Altogether, each side of the matter had its advantages and disadvantages, and a decision was hard to arrive at.

Two considerations weighed the balance in favour of going to Leipzig. One was that there Moscheles would be in closer contact with his friend Mendelssohn. (How could he know that Mendelssohn was to die within a year ?) The other was that while he was growing rather old for the life of a concert virtuoso, the world of piano playing was clearly passing him by.

Moscheles was one of the wise performers who will not drag out an old age on the platform. As early as 1839, when he was but forty-five, he wrote in his diary : " How delightful it would be to retire in the full tide of popular favour, in full consciousness of powers ! " He recognized more and more as time went on that the new school and he were antipathetic, and indeed fundamentally opposed. In 1839 he had said that " should the world take less interest in his performances as an executant, his desire would be the more ardent to cultivate music in accordance with his own taste and convictions." The world still regarded him warmly in 1846, and he might have gone on without change for a long while; but probably it seemed to him that, by teaching quietly in the Conservatorium, he would be able to propagate his ideas better than by further wandering the world as a pianist or teaching at home in a private capacity: his pupils would go forth armed with his armour, and bearing the great authority of the School.

When it was known that Ignaz Moscheles was about to leave London, musicians began to ask if some post of honour and profit could not be found him in this country, so that the distinction of his living here should not be lost. It was pointed out how excellently he had served the Philharmonic Society from the time he had triumphantly produced the Choral Symphony of Beethoven. The musical world was reminded that for many years he had been one of the most high-minded concert-givers in the city. (It was Moscheles who first dared to give a Piano Concert without the orchestra attending.) But there was no post for him in England, and so Leipzig received him.

IX

There is nothing of importance to relate in connection with the twenty-four years spent in Leipzig. Moscheles at once became one of the chief musicians in the place, visited invariably by all strangers who came there for any artistic purpose. His pupils did not include any of the great pianists of that or the next generation, the stream of high talent flowing towards the master of the new style, Liszt. Moscheles played abroad as the spirit moved him; he lectured, and composed continually; and he did all in his power to help young people, until he died, aged seventy-six, in the year 1870.

George Henschel became a Moscheles pupil in 1867. In his " Musings and Memories of a Musician " (1918), Sir George gives us an account of Moscheles at that time which I copy here, for the reason that it gives a living picture of the last of the pre-Lisztian virtuosos in his old age :

    . . . Moscheles' name had been familiar to me from his studies for the pianoforte, and in being introduced to him I felt a certain sensation of awe on shaking the hand of one who had seen Beethoven face to face, and had been commissioned by the master to prepare the vocal score of his *Fidelio*.

My lessons with Moscheles proved highly interesting and profitable, and sometimes amusing as well. He had been trained in, and was the foremost exponent then of, a school of pianoforte-playing as far removed from the modern sledge-hammer clavier technique as Mr. Oliver Wendell Holmes' "one-horse-shay" from a sixty-horse-power motor. I think the dear old gentleman would have had a fit if any of us pupils had forgotten ourselves so far as to lift our hands as much as two inches above the keyboard. Chopin and Schumann were the most advanced composers he admitted for study in his lessons, and I remember well, playing once a phrase of Beethoven's in a somewhat rubato style, his gently chiding me and innocently saying, " My dear sir, you may do that with Schumann or Chopin, but not when you play Beethoven or *me* ! "

On another occasion I brought him, for his criticism, a pianoforte composition of my own, of which he had accepted the dedication. After he had made a slight change or two I asked him if I now should play to him the corrected version. " My dear sir," he said with a smile, " there's no need for that, I hear it all in my mind's ear—I really must tell you a little story about that. When I wrote

212

my concerto with three kettle-drums "—he
seemed to feel a particular pride and satisfaction in remembering this then almost
unheard-of boldness and revolutionary innova-
tion—" when I wrote my concerto with three
kettle-drums, I came to a ' tutti ' which I
wanted rather fully and noisily orchestrated.
Well—will you believe, I heard that tutti and
the noise of the different instruments so
distinctly whilst I was writing it, that—*that I
got a headache !* "

x

Another picture of Moscheles, now from the
autobiography of Sir Charles Halle, shows us
Moscheles twenty-five years earlier, when he
would be less than fifty years old, but settled
already into that charming fussiness which
marked his nature. This second extract, while
showing the insistent care he had for his music,
rather indicates that his " mind's ear " was not
so active as the first extract implies :

. . . Moscheles had often been at my house
in Paris, even daily during the few months
which he spent there, occupied with the composition of his second pianoforte sonata for
four hands [the Op. 112]. I have indeed
reason to remember that sonata, for whenever
he had added twenty or twenty-four bars to
the unfinished work, he came to see me with

the beautifully written manuscript to try them over. And in order to give them their due effect, as he said, we had always to begin from the introduction and to go through the whole sonata until the new portion was reached, so that for every twenty new bars in the finale, we played the introduction, the allegro, the andante, the scherzo, and the finale, so far as it was ready. Often I was fetched from my house even as late as midnight by the amiable and charming Madame Moscheles, because " they had a few friends with them who were anxious to hear the sonata." I must have played it a few hundred times in this mutilated way before, on its completion, Moscheles gave a grand evening party at Kalkbrenner's house to produce it before the artistic and literary world. It met with success, but has never eclipsed the first sonata, which remains superior to it in freshness of ideas. I am still glad that I never showed any signs of impatience during this long trial; ever since I battled as a boy with Moscheles' " Variations sur la Marche d'Alexandre," and his G minor concerto, I had venerated his name, and felt happy and proud to be chosen by and associated with him on this occasion.

In similar fashion had Moscheles taken every portion of the *Fidelio* piano score to Beethoven as it was finished, back in the year 1814.

MOSCHELES

The *Variations on the March of Alexander*, written in 1815, when Moscheles was twenty-one, had by its success made him famous. The piece spread over Europe, and to the end of his days he had to play it, whether he wanted to or not, and long after he was tired of it.

Ignaz Moscheles, living the first years of his life among a public whose tastes were low, became inevitably a purveyor of banal music. The habit fixed, he continued such making of fashionable pieces. His Op. 58 (to take the piece that first strikes my eye as I look at a list of his compositions) is a " Gigue and Quadrille Rondo " entitled *Jadis et Aujourd'hui.* His Op. 72 is a set of " Fantasies Dramatiques " *in the Italian style, on favourite airs by Pasta, Sontag, and Malibran.* Other works are " Charms of London " or of Paris. But from the beginning he strove to make good music as well as modish music, being, as I said, a dual-natured man, born (unfortunately for his talent) out of time. The Study in B minor, Op. 70, is worthy of Schumann; there is a *Ballade* in A minor which is of true " character "; and a careful search through his three or four hundred works would yield a number of pieces of interest even to-day.

He was the perfect maker of music, as distinct from the master of music. If all the virtuosos had been controlled by the same idealism, their

world would have been a different place. But
they were for the most part touched, and more
than touched, by the spirit of showmanship, and
their natures were small, being crossed by
jealousy and self-seeking. They lived for the
profit of the passing moment, and had their reward.

In Moscheles, however, was something of
nobility, which supported a loving spirit of gentleness and kindliness. It is pleasant to know
that his epoch closed with him, and not with
a Kalkbrenner or a Steibelt.

III. SINGERS

To URSULA GREVILLE

XIX THE FIRST SINGERS

1

SINGING did not exist as a pure art before the rise of modern music. It was not cultivated as a thing sufficient unto itself. Men sang, and they sang in every country and in every generation, according to the general condition of music ; but they did not sing solely to produce beauty.

Modern music arose with opera, and so the Art of singing dates from the half-century between 1600 and 1650.

In earlier times both sacred and secular singing were in use. Troubadours, and the minnesingers, and also the natural vocalists among the peasantry, made the secular song; and church choristers made the sacred. Technique was very elaborate: we know that every church supporting a choir maintained a school in which the choristers were trained and instructed; some of the florid music of mediæval times is hard for even a clever singer of to-day; yet all this work was directed to a purpose other than that of pure art—the secular musicians sang to tell a story or celebrate an event, and the sacred musicians sang for the service of the church. Lovely tone, and the executive technique which is a joy in itself, were not cultivated, or even thought of. Men had only to sing in time and to tune. No one minded if they shouted or languished; and in all probability the sounds they made were as coarse as those of early organs or the first wind instruments.

Writers on music who lived in those remote days generally name a few famous singers, much as a writer to-day would mention Caruso and Tetrazzini; but they tell us nothing of the personality of the singers, and so it is but a pleasant fancy to try to revive such a man as Makeblite of Winchester, who lived in England before the year 1300, or such a man as Blakismet, who sang in the court of King Henry the Second.

Was this Blakismet a blacksmith, and if he was, did he win to fame from a lowly trade by the aid of exceptional ability, good fortune, and that tact which a court demands ? It would be pleasant to have a work of historical fiction invented around this man.

II

The term "*bel canto*" stands for vocal virtuosity and beauty of tone. The art it denotes flourished unduly for more than two hundred years. Gluck reformed opera by modifying the use of the *bel canto* in music drama, and Wagner substituted that "*declamation*" which made his music so hard for the great Italian singers of the latter part of the nineteenth century; but the *bel canto* still remains, and when it is combined with the high poetic intelligence of Wagnerian declamation it becomes one of the chief elements of the art of music, the equal of the string quartet and solo violin, and in the minds of many persons the superior of those two elements.

Walter's prize-song, in *The Mastersingers*, is a model of *bel canto* and just declamation.

Giulio Caccini, one of the Florentines who invented recitative, and with recitative opera, was the first musician of the modern world to lay down a method of singing, and thus to convert singing into an art. This method was his *Le nuove musiche*, published in 1602.

He was a charming singer, very famous in northern Italy, and a teacher who sent his art forward into the next generation by means of perfectly trained pupils. It is particularly observed that Caccini taught variation of tone, directing the singer to move from loud to soft according to the sentiment of the piece. Italian writers around the year 1650 used to say that " the new and graceful manner of singing, which at the beginning of the century spread itself over Italy," arose directly from Caccini and from Jacopo Peri, who with Caccini wrote the first of all operas in the year 1594.

One of these Italian writers, Pietro della Valle, wrote in 1640 a long letter to a friend, in which he makes a thorough survey of the art of music at that time. In one part of his letter he speaks of the singers in the old manner, naming (among others heard by him in his youth) Ottaviuccio,

Verovio, Orazietto, and Giovanni Luca, the latter a man who sang a falsetto that reached up into the clouds : " However," he says, " these singers were very deficient in the requisites of good singing, trills, graces, and good direction of the voice excepted; they were deficient in *piano* and *forte*, in the swelling and diminishing of the voice by minute degrees, in expression, in helping the poet by attending to the sense and passion of the words, and in rendering the tone cheerful, pathetic, tender, bold, or gentle at will."

III

Composers in those first days of modern music were the chief performers of their own music, and they wrote according to their personal gifts of execution: if they could manage a certain kind of run or decoration, they brought it into the piece. A musician named Gagliano said no one could form any idea of the character of the new music, or imagine its effect on the listener, until it was heard from the mouth of the composer.

John Dowland, the English musician who was so famous in his day that poets did him honour, was as famed for singing as for composing.

Composers used also to write pieces to suit the special abilities of their pupils; this, indeed, went so far that the writer of an opera would allow certain numbers to be supplied by the teacher of one of the actors, so that the actor could fully display his or her powers.

Naturally the composers thought highly of the performers. They respected their critical judgment: Peri, for example, tells us that he felt himself honoured when Vittoria Archilei, called *Euterpe* for the beauty and intelligence of her singing, expressed her approval of his opera *Euridice*. Francesca Caccini, called by the people of her time *La Cecchina*, won their respect as poet and composer almost as fully as she won it by her singing.

Pietro della Valle talks to his friend of many women who seem to have been true artists, as we to-day apply the term : Signora Maddalena and her sister; Signora Adriana and her two daughters, Leonora and Caterina; and many others, whose names are thus preserved through a pleasant letter from a man to his friend.

IV

History contains plenty of stories of the pride and arrogance that, almost immediately, developed in operatic singers, and several men and women remain known simply because of the annoyance they were.

The earliest to win such a survival is Domenico Aldegati, who some time after the year 1633 insulted the composer Monteverde in the Piazza di San Marco, in Venice. Monteverde was then an old man; he had recently been admitted into an order of the priesthood, and for twenty years had been chief musician in the cathedral. We know of this incident, and so know of Domenico Aldegati, by reason of a letter Monteverde wrote, in which he says he complains of the insult not as priest, becase a priest can pardon everything, but as *maestro di capella*, which is an office of so great a dignity that its occupier cannot allow himself to be treated rudely and not protest.

Perhaps Aldegati was drunk at the time; if not, he was a swaggering impertinent.

XX. SIFACE, BALDASSARE FERRI, NICOLINI GRIMALDI

I

Among the many singers born in Italy in the second half of the seventeenth century, is the man known by the name Siface, or Sifacio. His proper name was Giovanni Francesco Grossi; but early in his life as a performer in opera he won great fame in a part representing Syphax, and from being referred to as *Il Sifacio* he acquired the name Siface to the exclusion of the other. We do not know what the opera was, or where it was produced; but the occasion must have been very conspicuous.

He was an artificial soprano, as were a large number of other singers between 1600 and 1750. The records say that his voice was powerful and of beautiful tone, and that his manner of singing was most expressive, having nobility, breadth, and fine poetic intelligence.

This artist was in London around the year 1687, and though the town contained many similar visitors from Italy, he stood apart from all by virtue of his musical gifts and general intelligence. Pepys got to know him, and invited him to his house. The diarist had closed down his secret record nearly twenty years before, and so there is no reference to Siface in Pepys; but Evelyn was there, and he notes the occasion in his diary under the date April 19th, 1687. On January 30th of the same year Evelyn heard

225

Siface sign in the Royal Chapel. When the
singer left England (about 1689), his departure
aroused a warm regret; so much so that a song
was published—to an air by Purcell—called
Sefauchi's Farewell.

Siface would be about thirty-eight when he
ended his visit to this country. Ten years later
he was travelling from Bologna to Turin, and
on the journey his postillion murdered him for
the wealth he was carrying.

II

Siface's fame, however, seems to have been
almost small by comparison with the fame of
another male soprano. This artist, born in
1610, and therefore about forty years older than
Siface, was named Baldassare Ferri. He was
the great favourite of kings and queens, and of
all rulers under whom he served.

At the age of fifteen he was taken from Italy
to Poland by Prince Vladislas, where for forty
years he was attached officially to the court.
He then entered the service of the Emperor of
Germany, remaining there for ten years. The
Emperor Leopold covered him with honours;
more than this, he hung his portrait in his bedroom
crowned with a wreath of laurel, and inscribed
Baldassare Perugino, Re dei Musici. (Perugia was
Ferri's birthplace.)

At sixty-five, the singer craved to live his last

years in Italy. He gave up his post at the
German court, returned home, and died at Perugia
at the age of seventy.

His royal masters, unlike most employers of
their kind, had allowed him to travel abroad
freely. There is a report that once he was in
London, but no true evidence on the point.
At the age of thirty-three he was in Venice, when
the republic made him a knight of St. Mark.
He was honoured by the people of Florence and
other places, and about his fortieth year was
invited by the Queen of Sweden to visit her
country and sing to her. A medal was struck
in his honour, his head shown on one side, and
on the other a representation of the dying swan
on the banks of the Meander.

Ferri differed from most artificial tenors in the
respect that he sang with pathos as well as with
strength and brilliance. His breath control was
unique, and his voice almost miraculously agile.
He was finely cultured, and spoke well; and he
was a handsome man of dignified appearance.
Wealth came to him; but he lived quietly,
without display, and so when he died there was
much money to will away. Of this, more than
half a million crowns was left to a religious
foundation. We read of such a man, and try
to imagine the beautiful limpidity of his singing:
but we have no artificial male sopranos, and so
cannot form an idea of the quality of his art.
The last male soprano to sing in England was

named Velluti: he came here about 1825, and people found (not having heard a male soprano for a generation) that they did not now like such singers.

III

But neither Ferri nor Siface remains in so brilliant a light as Nicolini Grimaldi, who was in London for six or seven years, and whose art is frequently spoken of in the literature of the period. He was an artificial soprano, whose voice gradually became a contralto. The year of his birth is understood to be 1673, or thereabouts, and the place Naples. From 1694 to 1708 Grimaldi (or, as he is generally called, Nicolini) sang in opera in various Italian towns, winning great fame, and being decorated with the Order of St. Mark, Venice, which accounts for his title of the Cavaliere Nicolini; and then he came to London.

Italian opera was very fashionable in London at that time, and Italian singers were safe to make something like a fortune. This Italian came over without any assured engagement, but in the certain knowledge that it was safe for him to speculate on finding favour: this was in 1708. when Nicolini would be about thirty-five.

His confidence was immediately justified. He appeared on December 14th in an opera by Alessandro Scarlatti. The opera was *Pyrrhus and Demetrius*. It had been given in Rome ten or fifteen years earlier, and now was translated into English, with some additional songs by another composer resident in London ; but while the English members of the company sang in English, Nicolini and another Italian sang in Italian : such a confusion of tongues has not upset opera audiences until recently, and it persisted at Covent Garden until almost the end of the nineteenth century.

So great was Nicolini's success that he was engaged to sing for three years, at a yearly salary of eight hundred guineas. Among the operas in which he took part were several of which he wrote or adapted the plot and the text, for he was a fair poet: one of these was the piece which brought in a lion, and so was the occasion of Addison's raillery in *The Spectator*, March 15th and March 16th, 1711—it was entitled *Hydaspes*.

Nicolini left England in 1712, but sang here again in the years 1714, 1715, 1716 and 1717, travelling—as it seems—to and from London for the season. These were the years of Handel's first Italian operas, in some of which Nicolini appeared. We do not know when he died, but for several further years he continued his work in Italy.

IV

It was by acting no less than by singing that this man pleased the people and won the praise

229

of literary folk. Students of opera still argue about performance; one will say the singing must be the chief thing, another the acting, while a third will say that both singing and acting must be equally good. Some of our performers act well and sing badly, and *vice versa ;* we are pleased or irritated according to our own nature: but provided the artist knows how to sing, and can act well, it does not matter if his or her actual voice is poor, if only the piece is one of true dramatic character. Of course, in operas made simply and solely for vocal display, where the *bel canto* is the beginning and end of the art incorporated, the singer must be a perfect singer; but in such pieces true drama does not enter essentially: the persons in the play are puppets, and good acting is both uncalled for and impossible. In the days of Nicolini Grimaldi, when opera was in its first power and beauty, singing was the prime consideration, and students went so far as to doubt if the same individual could manage to act as well as to sing: says Pier Tosi, writing in 1723, " The mind being at once divided by two different operations, he will probably incline more to the one than the other; it being, however, much more difficult to sing well than to act well, the merit of the first is beyond the second. What a felicity would it be to possess both in a perfect degree ! "

It seems clear that Nicolini Grimaldi afforded that " felicity " to opera-goers in the days of his prime. Yet our English writers have more to say of his acting, first because it was the art that appealed to them most, and secondly because it was more rare in Italian opera—good actors though most of the Italians were.

Although few readers of these remarks will be without copies of *The Tatler* and *The Spectator*, I will copy here some of the comments made by Steele and Addison on Nicolini's acting. In *The Tatler*, No. 115, Steele reviews the production of the opera *Pyrrhus and Demetrius*, and delivers himself of the following extraordinary criticism :

> For my own part I was fully satisfied with the sight of an actor who, by the grace and propriety of his action and gesture, does honour to the human figure. Everyone will imagine that I mean Signor Nicolini, who sets off the character he bears in an opera by his action, as much as he does the words of it by his voice. Every limb and every finger contributes to the part he acts, insomuch that a deaf man may go along with him in the sense of it. There is scarce a beautiful posture in an old statue which he does not plant himself in, as the different circumstances of the story give occasion for it. He performs the most ordinary action in a manner suitable to the greatness of his character [in the play]; and shews the prince even in the giving of a letter, or dis-

patching of a messenger. Our best actors are somewhat at a loss to support themselves with proper gesture, as they move from any considerable distance to the front of the stage; but I have seen the person, of whom I am now speaking, enter alone at the remotest part of it, and advance from it with such greatness of air and mien, as seemed to fill the stage, and at the same time command the attention of the audience with the majesty of his appearance.

Steele was a good critic, and he had no call to advertise the genius of this Italian opera singer; rather, indeed, the reverse: but he generously makes us see that the man was a true dramatic artist, because it is only by real imaginative understanding that an actor can so create a part that he seems to be the character of that part in life. No acquired technical skill can fabricate an illusion. The actor who has only the mechanism of the matter is like the elocutionist who, with no understanding of poetry, tries to create the poetic substance of a piece by the artificial inflections and wailings of his conventionalized art. Nicolini must have been the born actor.

Addison says :

I have often wished that our tragedians would copy after this great master in action. Could they make the same use of their arms and legs, and inform their faces with as significant looks and passions, how glorious

would an English tragedy appear with that
action which is capable of giving a dignity
to the forced thoughts, cold conceits, and unnatural expressions of an Italian opera.

Thus Addison and Steele both inform us
that our acting on the English dramatic stage was
inferior to the acting of men like Nicolini Grimaldi
on the Italian operatic, despite of the dual nature
of the latter.

Steele and Addison suffered by the popularity
of Italian opera, for each was interested in the
spoken drama. And so when Nicolini left
England in 1712, Steele was glad, and delivered
himself of the following poem :

Begone, our nation's pleasure and reproach !
Britain no more with idle trills debauch :
Back to thy own unmanly Venice sail,
Where luxury, and loose desires, prevail ;
There thy emasculating voice employ,
And raise the triumphs of the wanton boy [*i.e.*,Cupid]
Long, ah ! too long, the soft enchantment reigned,
Seduced the wise, and even the brave enchained :
Hence with thy curst deluding song ! Away !
Shall British freedom thus become thy prey,—
Freedom which we so dearly used to prize
We scorned to yield it, but to British eyes ?
Assist, ye gales, with expeditious care !
Waft this preposterous idol of the fair !
Consent, ye fair, and let the trifler go,
Nor bribe with wishes adverse winds to blow.
Nonsense grew pleasing with his syren arts,
And stole from Shakespeare's self our easy hearts

XXI CATHERINE TOFTS &
MARGHERITA DE L'EPINE

ENGLISH singers in the days of Nicolini were as popular as the Italian, and they seem to have sung equally well. Indeed, some of the English-women could command a higher salary ; for example, Mrs. Anastasia Robinson (who had a thousand pounds a season, with in addition a benefit performance) and Mrs. Catherine Tofts.

Anastasia Robinson sang chiefly between 1714 and 1724. She was born about 1698. Her father was a portrait painter ; he became blind, and Anastasia had to take to opera singing to support him and the rest of the family. She married the Earl of Peterborough, after experiences with him which were exactly the same as those of Samuel Richardson's Pamela.

I

Catherine Tofts was one of the first English singers who made profit of the popularity in London of Italian opera. Her stage life ended as early as the year 1709, and it had not lasted more than six or seven years. She had the ability to sing in the desired Italian manner; and while the managers of theatres were gathering together a body of native Italians (which took some time) she enjoyed a profitable career—" enjoyed " is the right word to use, because she was of a money-loving nature.

CATHERINE TOFTS

Her fate, however, was a sad one, for she became liable to attacks of insanity from the year 1709 onwards; though the chief reason of her leaving the stage was her marriage with Joseph Smith, who about that time was made English consul in Venice.

Mrs. Tofts was also one of the first pair of opera singers whose rivalry set a town by its ears. The object of her jealousy was a singer named Francesca Margherita de l'Epine.

II

Margherita was a woman of curious history. From 1692 she sang in England, and did not give up public work until she married Dr. Pepusch in 1718, to whom she brought savings that amounted to the sum of ten thousand pounds: she was an ugly woman, but so good a singer and actress that her bad looks did not interfere with her success. She died in 1746, at what must have been a fairly advanced age.

Margherita sang for the first time at Drury Lane in the end of January, 1704. When she sang for the second time, which was a few days later, there was a disturbance in the theatre; and the rumour got about that this was prompted by Catherine. The rumour may, or may not, have been founded on truth, because in those days singers used to labour hard to spoil the work ot a rival; but Catherine, probably fearing that the report would do her no good, wrote a letter for publication to the editor of a newspaper, in which she says :

> Ann Barwick having occasioned a disturbance at the theatre-royal, Drury Lane, on Saturday night last, the 5th of February, and being thereupon taken into custody, Mrs. Tofts, in vindication of her innocency, sent a letter to Mr. Rich, master of the said theatre, which is as followeth : Sir, I was very much surprised when I was informed that Ann Barwick, who was lately my servant, had committed a rudeness last night at the play-house, by throwing of oranges, and hissing when Mrs. L'Epine, the Italian gentlewoman, sung. I hope no one can think that it was in the least with my privity, as I assure you it was not. I abhor such practices; and I hope you will cause her to be prosecuted, that she may be punished, as she deserves. I am, sir, your humble servant,
>
> KATHARINE TOFTS.

The town wits made plenty of fun out of this and the subsequent events; and they and the poets followed the two singers with smart epigrams and cynical verses; all of which was good publicity for the artists. Those relating to Margherita cannot be copied here, since they

would not be altogether clear without a full
account of the lively circumstances of her life.

III

Catherine was avaricious; she pressed her
manager, Mr. Rich, for the utmost farthing of
expenses in connection with performances of
opera; and at a social gathering she would allow
the gentlemen to kiss her at the rate of a guinea
a kiss: she was a very beautiful woman, the entire
opposite of Margherita, and of the gentlemen
present at these gatherings (so Lady Wentworth
tells us, in a letter dated March 17th, 1709)
" some took three, others four, others five at
that rate, but none less than one."
 And so a verse-maker wrote :

> So bright is thy beauty, so charming thy song,
> As had drawn both the beasts and their Orpheus
> along :
> But such is thy avarice, and such is thy pride,
> That the beasts must have starved, and the poet
> have died.

Her insanity, removed for a while by careful
treatment, returned in later years. Joseph Smith,
her husband, maintained a great house in Venice,
of which a retired part was reserved for her use;
there was a large garden attached to the house,
and here Catherine would walk for many hours,
either melancholy, or fancying herself back on

the stage, in which mood she would sing snatches of the old lays. This went on until 1735 or later, and then she died.

In *The Tatler* for May 26th, 1709, is a cruel account of her first fit of madness, written by Richard Steele.

XXII. SENESINO: AND CUZZONI AND FAUSTINA

AROUND Handel in London cluster an amazing group of singers, whose names are almost as significant as the names of his operas. But, indeed, the same is to be said of every great writer of opera; and when we extend our general reading beyond the first main facts of history, it is good to learn carefully of the work and character of performers, because these not only joined composer and public, but in various ways influenced the actual making of the music.

Art is regularly conditioned by the means at disposal for its presentation; that is, in music, for example, the creator in such an art as opera is always inclined to make special use of the gifts —mental and physical—of the available singers, and so we understand his work better by knowledge of those for whom it was immediately planned. (These remarks apply chiefly to ordinary business opera, of course, not to music-drama of the Wagnerian kind : this last is not business opera, but true art, like the Bach fugue and Beethoven symphony.)

I

Handel had trouble with some of his singers, in particular with an artificial soprano known as Senesino, so named because he was a native of Siena.

239   Q

MAKERS OF MUSIC

This man, properly Francesco Bernardi, whose delivery of *recitative* was finely intelligent, was born in or about 1680. Handel met him in Dresden, where Senesino was singing at the court theatre, and engaged him for his London opera at a salary of fifteen hundred pounds. This was in 1720. For some years matters ran fairly smoothly, but gradually trouble developed.

The outcome of the trouble was the ruin of Handel's operatic business, his bankruptcy, and this composer's ultimate work in oratorio: thus but for Senesino and the party he represents we might never have had *The Messiah* and *Judas Maccabæus*.

It was the conceit of the singer that brought about the trouble. The strange excitement with which ordinary people approve of a singer surrounded him, and he guessed he was a very important man indeed. Handel, however, put a performer in a less lofty state; he knew what a performer was worth, and the relative values of interpreter and creator. But where Senesino was a tactful man with his worshippers, Handel was not a tactful man with his singers: he actually swore at them when their tantrums and conceits interfered with good straightforward work, and when their nervous concern for self-display made them dissatisfied with his music; and to swear at a singer whom the money-spending populace adore seems an awful thing to a mind like that of Senesino.

SENESINO

Unpleasant conditions were possible from the moment the singer got to London; they developed rapidly after 1729; and eventually the composer refused to have him in the company. The nobility and gentry said, Either Senesino or no support from us. Handel made his rejoinder in asterisks; and the opposition set up that rival opera which, in the end, defeated Handel (and at the same time ruined itself).

In 1735 Senesino went back to Italy, with his savings (£15,000); he built a large house in Siena, and after a while died. Many stories accompany his name: one is that in the performance of an opera where Senesino played the part of Julius Cæsar, a piece of machinery fell upon the stage just as the actor was declaring that Cæsar knew not fear; the accident startled him, he fell a-trembling, began to cry, and could not go on with the play until assured that the danger was over.

II

Still more distracting was the trouble that attended on the work of Francesca Cuzzoni and Faustina Bordoni.

Cuzzoni is the singer Handel threatened to throw out of the window if she made any more hindrances at rehearsal. She had a high voice, clear and sweet, and that kind of pathetic expression which (aided in her case by an air of naïveté and innocence) is likely to move sensitive people to tears. Her rhythmical understanding was perfect; and to a thorough command of *crescendo* and *diminuendo* she added the last essential grace of performance, which is a perfectly proportioned *tempo rubato*—an element that grows of a sense of just time and of a fine general intelligence.

They say she was not a good actress, however; that mostly she looked cross and vexed; and that she dressed her insignificant body ungracefully. By nature she was capricious, and by circumstance she became intolerably self-willed.

It was in 1722 that she came to London to sing for Handel and his directors, when twenty-two years old. Her success was immediate, and soon other women singers gave up trying to stand against her popularity.

From 1723 to 1726 Cuzzoni reigned without a rival. Handel was more than usually careful to write music exactly suited to her voice and style; and matters would have gone on with entire satisfaction but for her discontent and never-ending presumption. Senesino's example of independence and opposition turned her head, which was always more than a little silly ; and at last Handel had to bring in someone else to help him to make a stand against her. He selected Faustina Bordoni, a singer seven years older than Cuzzoni, and very famous in Italy, where she wielded enormous personal power over the public, and was much honoured by great persons.

Faustina was handsome, graceful, a good actress, with fine facial expression and a true sense of drama. Her articulation of words was surprisingly rapid; and though she does not seem to have had the delicate " free time " of Cuzzoni, her command of time was still good, and she could sing words and phrases with true poetical character—this last is rather a rare gift in singers.

Faustina's breath-control was superb ; the records state that she could sustain a note longer than any other singer, and that her breathing was imperceptible. Her manner was polite, and she was instinctively courteous; always excepting when in contact with Cuzzoni.

III

These two had already sung on the same stage, in Venice in the year 1719. There was probably no sweetness wasted between them even at that time; but now, in 1726, and in London, all was bitterness. Their salary was equal—£2,000 a year ; and their opportunities were equal. The directors originally intended the two to work to mutual profit, the one singer by contrast enabling the other to shine to finer advantage, though Handel himself had other intentions; but the animosity of the two women was native—they simply detested each other.

This mutual hatred became malicious. One slandered the other in private, and in public abused her; the other retaliated, and as neither was the superior in this miserableness, their rage grew until when they met in person they fought— with scratches, pinches, kicks and hair-pulling, and I have no doubt verbal expressions which even Handel would rather have listened to behind a screen.

Operatic London divided into two camps, the men for the most part supporting Faustina, for she was beautiful. Some of the women who supported Francesca went so far as to imitate her ugly way of dressing herself on the stage, which shows how fatally they were in earnest.

On the one side, Cuzzoni's, were Lady Walpole, the Countess of Pembroke, Sir Wilfred Lawson, Sir William Gage, Simon Smith, etc., etc.; on the other Sir Richard Walpole, Lady Delawar, the Countess of Burlington, etc., etc.

The theatre divided, and when one singer sang, her supporters applauded and her opponents hissed; then when the other singer sang, the halves of the audience changed over the nature of their activities. This exercise of the typical English coolness and restraint put an end to opera for a little while; and at last the directors agreed with Handel that Cuzzoni must go.

Cuzzoni had sworn (literally, and not merely

in the way of emphatic statement) that she would not accept a smaller salary than Faustina. So when the date arrived for a renewal of contracts, the management fixed Faustina's salary at a guinea higher than Cuzzoni's. The latter had taken her oath on the Bible. She could not retract, and so she departed.

Among the poor bits of verse that accompanied her departure was the following effusion from the pen of Ambrose Phillips :

> Little syren of the stage,
> Charmer of an idle age,
> Empty warbler, breathing lyre,
> Wanton gale of fond desire,—
> Bane of every manly art,
> Sweet enfeebler of the heart,—
> O, too pleasing is thy strain :
> Hence, to southern climes again !
> Tuneful mischief, vocal spell,
> To this island bid farewell ;
> Leave us as we ought to be,—
> Leave the Britons rough and free.

IV

Faustina remained with Handel until the break-up of his main operatic enterprise (1733). Then she went to Dresden and married the composer Johann Adolf Hasse. She worked in the Dresden opera until 1751, in such esteem that when she gave up the stage her full salary was continued for another twelve years.

Political troubles, in which her husband's manuscripts were burned, drove them from Dresden to Vienna: here, it appears, they lived until 1775, when they removed to Venice, the city where Faustina was born, and where she died in 1783, at the age of ninety, more than a half-century after those years in London. I shall have something to say of her life in Vienna in a moment.

v

Francesca Cuzzoni, one of those people who carry trouble with them, because they weave it out of themselves every day, had a miserable close. She came back to England to sing for the opposition-opera which ruined Handel; and then, about the year 1749, she came here a third time : "I was at this concert myself," says Burney, "and found her voice reduced to a mere thread; indeed, her throat was so nearly ossified by age that all the soft and mellifluous qualities, which had before rendered it so enchanting, were nearly annihilated, in her public performance; though I have been assured by a very good judge, who frequently accompanied her in private, that, in a room, fine remains of her former grace and sweetness in singing Handel's most celebrated songs, by which she had acquired the greatest reputation, were still discoverable."

So much for the decay of her art, which was

FRANCESCA CUZZONI
SANDONI

SIGNORA
FAUSTINA

inevitable. But there was a worse decay in store for this unhappy woman. Her " turbulent and obstinate temper " did not decay, nor her " extravagance and caprice." Leaving England for the last time, she went to Holland. There she got into debt, and was imprisoned for the same. The keeper of the prison allowed her to sing occasionally in public, by which means she earned enough to pay off the debt: one of his warders accompanied her to and from the concert place. Then she made her way to Bologna. Her poverty was extreme, and it descended into squalor as during the last few years of her life she earned a few shillings a week by covering buttons with silk.

Francesca Cuzzoni was seventy when she died, in absolute destitution. In the days of her pride she had " *begged of an English nobleman a suit of lace, but not liking it when sent to her, she threw it into the fire.*"

VI

We can visit Faustina in her home at Vienna, and see what a different old age was attained to by the rival of Francesca.

Forty years have gone by; Handel has been dead more than ten years; the greater part of Gluck's work is done, though his finest operas are not yet written; Haydn is famous; the boy Mozart is known the world over; and Beethoven

is a child a year or two old. It is with Burney
that we see Faustina, for he paid her and her husband several calls during his tour on the Continent, in the year 1772.

I copy the following from Burney's *Present
State of Music in Germany, the Netherlands, and
United Provinces.*

" This morning, the Abate Tarussi was so
obliging as to return my visit. He had already
run over my book, and was sufficiently apprized
of my pursuits; after a long conversation at my
lodging, he carried me to Signor Adolfo Hasse,
who lives in a handsome house in the suburbs,
called the Landstrass. Signora Faustina was at
the window, and seeing us stop at the door came
to meet us; I was presented to her by my conductor. She is a short, brown, sensible, and lively
old woman; said she was much pleased to see
a Cavaliere Inglese, as she had formerly been
honoured with great marks of favour in England.

" Signor Hasse soon entered the room; he is
tall, and rather large in size, but it is easy to
imagine that in his younger days he must have
been a robust and fine figure; great gentleness
and goodness appear in his countenance and
manners. He seems to have been more ill-
treated by time than Faustina, though he is
younger than her by ten years. . . . His two
daughters came in; they are about twenty-eight
or thirty years of age, well-bred and agreeable

FAUSTINA

in their manners, and discover, immediately, that great care has been taken of their education. They read English, and speak it a little. . . ."

And so we see Faustina, who was a favourite more than fifty years before with royal music-lovers, now with daughters on the verge of middle life.   Burney goes a second time to the house :

" We found all the family at home, and our visit was truely cheerful and social.   Signora Faustina is very conversable, and is still possessed of much curiosity concerning what is transacting in the world.   She has likewise good remains, for seventy-two, of that beauty for which she was so much celebrated in her youth, but none of her fine voice !   I asked her to sing—*Ah non posso ! hò perduto tutte le mie facoltà.*   Alas ! I am no longer able, said she; I have lost all my faculties. . . .

" One of the daughters has a sweet *soprano voce di camera* [what to-day we call a ' drawing-room voice '], of which the tone is delicate and interesting; the other has a rich and powerful *contralto* voice, fit for any church or theatre in Europe: both have good shakes, and such an expression, taste, and steadiness, as it is natural to expect in the daughters and scholars of Signor Hasse and Signora Faustina. . . . His daughters complain of want of practice, and say they hardly ever sing; for their father is always either ill or busy. . . .

" Faustina, who is a living volume of musical

history, furnished me with many anecdotes of her contemporary performers: she spoke much of Handel's great style of playing the harpsichord and organ when she was in England, and said she remembered Farinelli's coming to Venice, in the year 1728, and the rapture and astonishment with which he was then heard. . . ."

VII

The singer Farinelli was then living in a state of melancholy grandeur in his palace a mile outside Bologna. He was nearing his seventieth year, but another ten years remained of his portion of life. Burney had seen him a year or two earlier, when making his tour through France and Italy, and in his other book he tells us a good deal of him.

Farinelli was, in many respects, the greatest of all those defective and peculiar beings, the male sopranos, artificial sopranos, evirati, castrati, or singing eunuchs, as they were variously named; his story is interesting, and worth the telling at length, but here it can be no more than outlined.

XXIII. FARINELLI

FARINELLI's name was Carlo Broschi. He had an uncle named Farinelli, a well-known violinist, author (or at least adapter and promulgator) of the famous ' *Farinel's Ground,*' which forms the theme of Corelli's *Folies d'Espagne* ; and the singer probably took the violinist's name either to honour it further or to help himself by its associations: this was frequently done in those days, musicians adopting the names of patrons or teachers.

A brother of his, Riccardo Broschi, is slightly known in musical history as a composer in opera.

I

Carlo was born in Naples, in 1705. His master was Porpora, teacher of Senesino and other famous singers, and a composer who was engaged by the opposition-party to help to destroy Handel in London.

As a boy Carlo became well-known in southern Italy: he was then called Il Ragazzo, which means the young boy.   The climax of his early fame was reached in 1722, when he sang for the first time in Rome. Like all pupils of the school of Porpora, he had a brilliant technique, and all through his life no composer could write anything in the way of proper music which he could not sing better than an instrumentalist could play it. His voice was powerful, wider in range than was usual with a male soprano, and miraculously agile. On this occasion of his debut in Rome, Porpora composed a duet for trumpet and solo voice, to be performed by Farinelli and a German trumpet virtuoso then in the city. The trumpet first gave out a long note, starting very soft, swelling to the utmost *forte*, and then returning to the quiet of the beginning, and retaining an immaculate purity of tone; the singer immediately echoed this, with greater length of note, more clear and pure tone, finer gradation in the *crescendo* and *diminuendo*, and a more extreme softness and loudness: then the trumpet entered upon brilliant runs, shakes, leaps, reiterations of the same note, and the like, which the voice either imitated or—taking up the pattern— overbore by its superior strength and staying power, so that in the end it was the dominant instrument.

We have to-day singers who compete in this manner with the flute, but not with the trumpet, because the Farinelli kind of vocalist is no longer manufactured.

History does not tell us anything about how the German trumpeter took his defeat; perhaps, like the bird in the Elizabethan poems that describe similar contests between singers and birds, he fell off his perch and died of a broken heart.

For eight or nine years Farinelli sang in all the great Italian cities, advancing day by day in

FARINELLI

fame. He worked hard, and never felt he had mastered all the art of bravura singing, but was always anxious to learn further. In 1727, when twenty-two years old, he met in contest a singer named Antonio Bernacchi, who was then about thirty-seven. Bernacchi, who had finely developed that art of embroidering a simple melody which in those days was the chief business of the *coloratura* singer, was known as Il Rè dei Cantatori. Being the junior, Farinelli sang first, and he sang with all that rapturous determination which seems a special gift of clever singers and most at command when they are put on their mettle. The audience went wild with enthusiasm, and then breathlessly awaited the response of the older master. This was nothing less than an exact repetition of what Farinelli had sung, with every run, turn, shake, pause, reiteration, and nuance. Bernacchi had heard the piece but this once; but he had the gift of a perfect memory— the memory which operates like a photographic plate; Mendelssohn had the same, and once similarly repeated a new piece of brilliant music played at a party by Liszt. I have already (on page 135) told how Bach repeated a once-heard piece.

Bernacchi was awarded the prize in the contest. Farinelli did not turn away in a huff and swear never to sing in the town again; on the contrary, he begged Bernacchi to give him lessons, which Bernacchi did, with, for result, a

253

final development of the younger man's executive powers.

Four years later the Austrian Emperor said to Farinelli that his art exhilarated the listener, moving him to astonishment and wonder, but that it did not touch the heart: he advised him to study expressive singing—the delivery, in simple manner, of a pathetic melody. Farinelli, with the wisdom that was eventually to keep him safe in the Spanish court for nearly a quarter-century, took the Emperor's recommendation; and in a short time the people discovered that their favourite in *bravura* was now their favourite in *espressivo*.

The story is told that early in this period of his life he and Senesino met for the first time in the same opera. Senesino was a tyrant king; Farinelli a poor captive in chains. In the play, the captive has to implore pity ; and this Farinelli did with such melting pathos that Senesino—despite the experience of rehearsals—forgot his character, and, shedding tears of sympathy, took his companion into his arms. There must have ensued a terrible scene of emotion in the theatre, for the Italian audiences always let themselves go when a direct and simple mood was expressed.

II

In 1734 Farinelli came to London, engaged by the party running the opposition-opera against

CARLO BROSCHI DETTO FARINELLI

Handel. He arrived with Porpora, and was
companioned by Senesino and Cuzzoni. The
newspapers announced his arrival as an event of
first importance; and before the opera performances began he was invited to call on the
King at St. James's Palace, where he sang to the
accompaniment of the Princess Royal.

Two such men as he and Senesino had never
been seen before in London opera. Senesino
had the lovelier tone, his body was graceful;
Farinelli was tall, and more than thin, he was
ungraceful in movement, and while singing stood
still as a statue. But Farinelli was seen to be
the greater marvel; and the town lost its head,
to an extent that would have surprised the
comparatively calmer Italians of the day.

The first note sung in public by Farinelli was
that long note with which he overcame the trumpet
in Rome. This was followed by rapid movement
and intricate articulation, which the violins could
not keep up with or imitate. But in between
the note and the rapid song was five minutes'
applause of the wildest kind.

Sometimes at a concert you see the singer
look reproachfully at the accompanist. This is
bad manners, except when the singer is the one
in fault; and then it is a wise and bold assertion,
which will deceive all but the knowing ones of
the audience. Farinelli had no such bad manners ; he was a modest gentleman. If the
accompanists, bewildered or outpaced, got con-

fused and broke down at rehearsal, he stopped, waited while they gathered themselves together, and then started again. He would wait even while they practised the movement at the particular spot that caused the trouble, and was always even-tempered.

This delicacy on the part of a master will strike some performers as absurd, and for certain it could not be cultivated by second-rate musicians.

Even clever instrumentalists had to train themselves to keep with him, and players who are well-known to students of musical history were as troubled as any other: among those who attended Farinelli's first rehearsal in London, and who broke down in his way, were Steffano Carbonelli, a favourite violinist who played here from 1720 to 1772; Michael Festing, a pupil of Geminiani; and Valentine Snow, the chief trumpeter of Handel's time.

III

The salary offered the singer was £1,500 a year, to which was added presents in money and jewelry to the yearly value of another £3,500. In three years he accumulated great wealth, because he did not squander money.

The presents received were advertised regularly in the *Court Journal* newspaper, and the nobility vied with one another in the magnificence

FARINELLI

of their gifts, much as they vied in the richness of their dress or the lavishness of their entertainments; while Farinelli retained his modest manner and kept a clear account of what he received.

Not only men and women of the aristocracy adored him and made of him a pet, but likewise the aldermen, their wives, and solid citizens generally. Such fascination after a while drew the anger of steadier persons: the more dignified writers began to implore Londoners to recollect the dignity of the country, which was famous abroad in commerce, arms and literature, and now was ridiculed for its wild infatuation.

At last Hogarth intervened (June 25th, 1735). The second plate of the " Rake's Progress " series gives a picture of the young wastrel's levee. Among the figures are Essex, the dancing-master, who receives a guinea for a ten-minutes lesson; the prize-fighter, Thomas Figg; an artist in gardening; a French fencing-master; a bugler; tailors and men-milliners; a bravo; a poor poet; a jockey; and others, among the latter a musician seated at a harpsichord and playing from an opera. The musician has come with a list of Farinelli's patrons, on which this young man is to inscribe his name and particulars of the present he gave the singer the other day, which is a splendid snuff-box, " chased with the story of Orpheus charming the brutes, value £100." The list hangs on the back of the chair by the harpsichord, spreading generously to the floor, until it reaches a picture of Farinelli on a pedestal, before him an altar bearing flaming hearts, and around the altar persons with extended arms offering gifts: one of the persons, a lady, is kneeling and saying *One God, One Farinelli*, in remembrance of the excited individual who from her box called out those words during the performance of a song by the Italian.*

The craze died; opera languished; presents diminished; and Farinelli left London for Paris, where he had a good public and social success, but nothing like that in London. He then went to Spain, in 1737, and at the age of thirty-two.

IV

King Philip the 5th of Spain was a dull, phlegmatic man, inclined to melancholia, which in its bad state made him want to abdicate the throne and refuse to be shaved. The former desire was a cause of worry to his wife, for she did not wish to be no longer a queen, nor did she wish to see the change in foreign policy which would

*Tye : Enough! let voices now delight his princely ear.
(*Then a song.*)
Prince Edward : Doctor, I thank you, and commend your
cunning :
I oft have heard my father merrily speak
In your high praise ; and thus his Highness saith :
' England one God, one truth, one doctor hath
' For music's art, and that is Doctor Tye,
' Admired for skill in music's harmony.'
—Samuel Rowley, *When you see me you shall know me* (a comedy : printed 1613).

come about if her husband retired. Therefore she tried by all means to modify his melancholy and to arouse him to a proper idea of things.

The latest plan was to bring Farinelli to the palace: the King had a sentimental fondness for nice singing, and this Italian, as all reports agreed, was the nicest in the world.

So Farinelli went to Madrid, intending to stay only a little while. The King was in a bad mood, and would not see him; for days he had not washed, changed or shaved: and there in his room he sat, a miserable, unhappy, pitiable man.

The Queen countered the King's refusal by arranging that Farinelli should go into a room adjoining the King's, and there sing some of his most expressive pieces. He did this; the King, hearing, was moved, and calling Farinelli to him, thanked him, gave him a present, and asked what other reward he would care for. Farinelli, obeying instructions, said that all he wanted was to see a king happy in carrying out his duties.

Caught thus in a mood of sentiment, Philip aroused himself. It was arranged that the singer should remain permanently attached to the court, at a salary of between £3,000 and £4,000 a year (with presents), and with servants and horses free of charge. His official duties were to regale the King with four pieces every evening; the task was not unpleasant, in itself, but as it was the same four songs every day that Farinelli had to

perform, the task must have got a trifle monotonous. Two of the songs were by Hasse ; another
was a minuet, which was given with variations.

This went on for ten years, or 3,652 days; and
the artist was content to do it. He was content
never to be a twelve-hours journey from the
palace. Was he lazy, to undertake such a service; or did he love the King ? Had he no true
ambition, or did he think it noble to sacrifice
ambition for the King's mental good ? Perhaps
it was that he liked the power attending upon his
peculiar office, and that politicians abroad wished
Farinelli to remain.

For Farinelli was able to influence Philip in
that particular policy which related to Spain,
France and Italy. He became the King's personal favourite, and his advice was asked and
followed. They made him a Knight of the Order
of St. Iago, and other honours followed.

Being prudent, quiet, and amiable, Farinelli
had no trouble with the courtiers. He assumed
nothing, was careful not to offend the dignity of
the proud Spanish nobles; and if he found a man
his enemy, went directly along the path that
would enable him to do that man a good turn.
It seems, indeed, that Farinelli was actually liked
by the entire general body of the Spanish court,
and that those who were opposed to the foreign
policy he supported did not care to try to injure
him. For this one admires him far more than for
that long note.

FARINELLI

Philip died in 1746, and his son reigned as
Ferdinand the 6th. Farinelli now was forty-one,
the new king thirty-three. Like his father,
Ferdinand was controlled by King Philip's wife
(who was not his mother, but his stepmother);
also he had the same melancholy, which yielded
to the same treatment. Therefore Farinelli
stayed on, though I have no doubt he was allowed
to change his programme. He became the new
king's first favourite, received more money and
honours, extended his political power, was made
knight of the proudest order in Spain—the
Order of the Cross of Calatrava (this was in 1750);
and still his life in the court was peaceful. Between them they established a fine opera, of which
Farinelli was manager, and to which he invited
many singers from Italy. Some of these he
taught, and so he now lived more vigorously in
his art.

v

After thirteen years, Ferdinand died. His
wife had died a little before; and his love for her
was such that he became distracted with grief:
for weeks he wandered about the palace, aban-
doned utterly to his melancholia; and the actual
hour of his dying was a terrible event.

Farinelli's occupation was now gone. The
other party came into power. The policy which
had been opposed for those twenty-three years
triumphed; and the singer was dismissed.

He left Spain in 1761, aged fifty-six, after a life there of twenty-five years. The Spanish government continued his great salary, on condition that he lived in Bologna and took no part in politics. Naples, his birthplace, was forbidden him, because Naples was the key-stone or centre of the new policy. Naturally Farinelli had no sentiment in this matter, either of his place of abode or of politics. And so he lived in a great *palazzo* a mile out of Bologna; entertaining guests in a quiet, friendly, and dignified manner; brooding over the past; and very glad to see Englishmen at any time (earlier in life he had named one of his houses—built out of his London fortune—*England's Folly*). He had a fine collection of clavichords, spinets, harpsichords, and other keyed instruments, among them a pianoforte made in 1730, of which he was proud. He had also a fine collection of pictures. These included portraits of his two Spanish kings; and often of an evening—perhaps every evening when he was alone—he sat gazing on these for hours, until his indulged melancholy relieved itself in tears. His death took place in 1782.

VI

A year later, and likewise in his own palace, died Caffarelli (Gaetano Majorano), another male soprano. This man had been odious and

CAFFARELLI

ridiculous all his long life of eighty years for covetousness and pride. He was in the beginning a beautiful peasant boy, in the end the Duke of Santo Dorato. It is this man of whom the story is told that his teacher, Porpora, kept him for five years on one page of exercises. He was very jealous of Farinelli; and once, when a prince told him he must do his best on a certain occasion, because Farinelli had recently sung in the same place, he said, "Have no fear. To-night you shall hear two Farinellis." Over the gate of his palace at Santo Dorato he had the inscription placed, *Amphion Thebas, ego domum.*

VII

Also in this year after Farinelli's death (1783) died Lucrezia Agujari, sometimes referred to as *Bastardella*, at the age of forty. She was famous for her high notes and facile execution. Mozart met her at Parma, in 1770, when she sang in his presence the following, which he noted down and sent home in the letter dated March 24th :

This I quote to show what the brilliant technicians of the eighteenth century could do. It also serves to remind us of the doubtful value of their abilities; no expression of thought or feeling is to be effected by such means, and so in the larger view this work was not art, except in the way of that art which is represented by

264

AGUJARI

the juggler who can balance two billiard balls
on a cue, and then balance the cue on his nose,
the while he lights a cigarette and takes a dozen
puffs. Mozart's father said in a letter, that
Agujari had at times a wild look in her eyes,
such as people have who are subject to convulsive
fits; and that she was lame. Burney, in his
History of Music (iv, 481), says that Agujari
got these high notes " in falset," and that " the
Danzi, now Madame Lebrun, went much higher
than the Agujari, in *real* voice, of the same
register as her middle notes.

" Such notes," he goes on, " may become a
canary-bird; but they are not human ": he says
that the singing of these notes is a trick, which
any good singer can learn, though not without
danger, as was shown in the case of a young man
named Lucca Fabris, who in struggling at a
high and difficult passage burst a blood-vessel,
and died of the hæmorrhage.

XXIV. TODI AND MARA

THIS year of 1783, in which died Caffarelli and Agujari, is famous in the history of singers for a war in Paris—a war quite as intense as that between Faustina and Cuzzoni spoken of on page 244. It was a swift war, bursting suddenly upon the (comparative) calm of Paris, and raging for a shorter period than the earlier one in London: it was not accompanied by feminine fisticuffs; but it divided Paris into two camps, and the members named themselves Maradists or Todists according as they supported the singer Mara or the singer Todi.

One of the pair was a German—the first great singer to come of Germany; the other was a Portuguese. The lines of their lives met in Paris, in this year of 1783; they had crossed at various points in the operatic maze, and were to cross again at other points in the years following the war: but the women died far apart, one right up north on the shores of the Gulf of Finland, the other south in Lisbon.

And they died in the same year, namely, 1823; the one almost as distracted as Cuzzoni, who covered buttons with silk in her last years; the other in the peace of a long married life. But the one who died in distress had not become obscure like Cuzzoni; on the contrary, two books were written about her when she was nearly eighty, and the greatest poet in Germany sent her a poem for her eightieth birthday.

TODI AND MARA

I

The unhappy member of this pair was Mara. She was born in Cassel, the capital city of the Electorate of Hesse-Cassel.

Cassel was a famous town, then as now. It stands on the river Fulda, with its famous schools, great museum and library, and many public institutions. When Gertrude Elizabeth Schmeling, afterwards "*the Mara*," was born, it was not controlled by Frederick II, King of Prussia ; but while she was a girl it passed into his hands, and Gertrude eventually entered his service. The town was always a good place for music; it was here that Spohr at one time lived, conducting the famous orchestra and teaching it to play to a baton. This, however, was not till seventy years after Elizabeth was born.

Johann Schmeling, her father, was a professional musician of no particular ability or position. In fact, he had to make his living partly by mending broken violins and other stringed instruments, and so was like our pianoforte teachers who add to their income by tuning pianos at four shillings a time.

Gertrude Elizabeth was born in February, 1749. The mother died almost immediately, and the father was left with the baby. His circumstances were very bad; when business took him out, he had to lock the child in a room, and during the hours when he was at work he had to tie her in an arm-chair, so that she should not crawl and tumble about and hinder him or upset his materials.

This constriction had a cruel effect on Gertrude. It made her rickety, very weak, and afflicted her with several bodily deformities, out of which it seems, she never grew.

The child was left alone nearly the whole of the first three or four years of her life. Her chief amusement was to watch the pendulum of a clock, figuring out the mystery of measured time and marking it by movements of the hand. Once, when sitting in a window, she surprised her father by beating time to a street musician who was playing on a guitar; but this did not cause him to suspect she was particularly musical. Nor did he suspect it when she picked up a violin he had mended and—plucking at it guitar-fashion—broke the strings. He was, indeed, angry with the meddlesome young monkey, and said he would punish her if she touched the instruments again.

However, little Gertrude kept her eyes open and watched her opportunities, and actually taught herself to play a scale on the violin, using the bow in such a manner as to produce true notes and a pure tone.

At first Johann Schmeling was angry again when he discovered this ability in the child, for it was the fruit of disobedience; but after a while he relented, and tried giving her some lessons.

To his surprise, she so swiftly mastered the business of violin playing that within a week or two she could take part in easy duets with him. She now was turned four, but still unable to walk.

Johann was naturally inclined to think that something might be done with this unexpected talent. He did not, like all parents of later years when thus apprised of genius in the family, think of the story of the child Mozart, because Mozart was not yet born; but he spoke of Elizabeth to music-lovers in Cassel, and invited some of them to hear his daughter.

II

One of the party thus assembled said she should be brought forward into the notice of the public: this man found the money to take Johann and the child to Frankfort (which is some eighty-five miles from Cassel), and there Elizabeth played at the Fair. The music-lovers of Frankfort were interested: they raised a subscription, the money to be expended on a musical and general education for the child, and on helping her to grow stronger in body; and so at the age of five this first of all juvenile wonders of the violin was safely started on her way.

Four years later Johann Schmeling took his daughter to Vienna. There they gave some concerts. The aristocracy, as was usual in those times, took up the cause of the curious little

269

musician; but opportunities, after all, were poor in Vienna, and on the advice of the English Ambassador, Johann determined to go to London. Probably the means were found by profits on the concerts, by the sale of presents, and by subscription. Gertrude could sing already, in a clear, strong voice, entirely untrained, of course, but miraculously in tune. Indeed, it did not seem possible for her to sing off the note.

London proved a good place. The Queen, and the ladies of the court, made much of the sickly little violinist; and though they did not approve of a female fiddler, they supported her by their patronage. (For a woman to play the violin in the middle eighteenth century was as unnatural as for a woman to play the French horn to-day.)

Elizabeth first played in London as one of a company of prodigies: here is the advertisement of the concert :

By Particular Desire. At the little Theatre in the Haymarket. This Day, April 23rd, there will be a Concert of Vocal and Instrumental Music. The vocal parts by Signor Tenducci, Signora Calori, and by Signor Qualici. The solos by young Performers, who never appeared in Public, as a solo of Signor Giardini's on the Violin by his scholar, Master Barron, thirteen years old ; a Lesson on the Harpsichord by Miss Burney, nine years old ; with a Sonata of Signor Giardini's

TODI AND MARA

*accompanied by a Violin ; a Solo on the Violoncello
by Master Cervetto, eleven years old ; a Duet on
the Violin and Violoncello by Master Barron and
Master Cervetto ; a Quartetto by Miss Schmeling,
Master Barron, Master Cervetto, and Miss
Burney. With several full Pieces by a select
Band of the best Performers.*

The year was 1760. The doors opened at
five, and the concert began at seven. (What
did the people who went at five do in the interval ?)
It cost half a guinea to sit in the pit and five
shillings in the gallery. You bought your
ticket at Mr. Walsh's music-shop, in Catherine
Street ; or at Mr. Johnson's music-shop, in
Cheapside; or at Arthur's, St. James' Street; or
at the Theatre. Ladies were desired to send
their Servants to keep Places in the Theatre.
. . . The Miss Burney was a daughter of the
historian, and thus a sister of the wonderful
person who wrote *Evelina* at twenty-five and is
now famous as Madame Frances D'Arblay,
though more often spoken of as Fanny Burney.
Of Master Barron I know nothing. The boy
Cervetto was a son of old " Nosey " Cervetto, the
'cellist and manager of Drury Lane, who died in
1783 at the age of 101, leaving £20,000 behind
him. Cervetto the Second was a great man
among the 'cellists of his time, and one of the
first to play with a singing tone. He died,
comparatively young, in the year Queen Victoria

271   S

came to the throne, failing to reach his father's age by no less than thirteen years.

III

And so little Elizabeth appeared in England as a prodigy violinist, one of a group of four clever children, in 1760, a year after the death of old Handel, and in the circles of the highest music-loving aristocracy.

Those ladies who were interested in her, among them the Queen, at once set to work to turn her from violin-playing. Her voice was fuller and stronger, and promised to be exceptional. Obeying a general advice, Johann Schmeling arranged for Gertrude to study singing. Paradisi (Paradies) was then living in London, and Gertrude was sent to him for lessons; but he was an eccentric, and not a man to whom girls could be safely entrusted, and the lessons did not continue long.

The Schmelings remained here till 1765, by when Gertrude was sixteen. Working hard, and mostly under her own guidance, she had made a fine singer of herself. But there was no opening in London, and therefore they went back to Germany, hoping to secure an engagement at the Court Opera of Frederick II.

In this they failed. The musical interests of Frederick the Great were Italian, as his literary interests were French, and though he had honoured Bach by that famous invitation to his court (out of which came the *Art of Fugue*), yet he was not inclined to support German musicianship, especially in the vocal departments.

Almost immediately Elizabeth won the high regard of J. A. Hiller, the Leipzig musician and great teacher of singing. She remained studying under him until the year 1771—that is, for five patient years, by the close of which she had so developed her genius that already she was regarded as the finest native singer in the country. Her voice was high; her technique was brilliant; better still, her knowledge of music was complete, for she was a born musician. (But when Mozart heard her, in 1780, he did not care for her singing, comparing her unfavourably with Agujari and Aloysia Weber.) Gertrude sang for Hiller at a concert in 1767, and Hiller could afford to pay her a fee of £85.

Her favourite music, now and for a long time after, was that of Hasse, the husband of Faustina. At present we do not use any of his works; in the eighteenth century he was one of the great men, ranking in general esteem with Handel and Bach, and sooner or later there will be a revival of interest in him, upon which a portion of his music will come back into use.

IV

Gertrude Schmeling sang in a Hasse opera,

at the Dresden Court Theatre. She was supremely successful; and King Frederick now gave her a post in his musical establishment.

The King was a genuine music-lover. In the mornings, while working at state affairs from five to eleven, he interluded his work with an occasional ten minutes of flute playing; he played well, and only gave it up when, later in life, he lost some of his front teeth. Then every evening, after the last set meal of the day, he had a concert.

Gertrude was engaged for life, signing a legal contract to remain attached to the Prussian court. This was an unwise thing to do, particularly with such an autocratic monarch. Her salary was about £425 a year.

Among the court musicians was an old Italian named Antonio Uberti, a pupil of Porpora, and known generally as Porporino. He was quite old, being seventy-four, but still retained his office of Chief Chamber Singer to the King. This man helped Gertrude to perfect her coloratura technique.

Also among the court musicians was a 'cellist named Mara—a dissipated man, hopelessly extravagant, and bad in every way. Gertrude fell in love with him, charmed by some romantic roguery in his manner. Twice they asked the King's permission that they might marry, each time being refused. At last they married in defiance, and there was much royal rage to endure.

This was a fatal act, and the cause of the bulk

of Gertrude's troubles in later life. She was now twenty-four, and not till she reached fifty did she separate from this poor handsome wretch. I have no doubt it was her life with him that continued her physical weakness; though she was not a particularly wise person herself, yielding to many infatuations, even when an old woman, and having many lovers. Her husband died in 1808, physically, morally and mentally a complete ruin of a man.

King Frederick took a dislike to his singer, now Gertrude Mara. He refused her even the little liberty that court musicians in those days could count on, and ceased to make allowance for illness. It is said that once, when she pleaded sickness as a reason for not appearing at a court concert, he sent an officer and a body of soldiers to her rooms, by whom she was taken out of bed and carried to the King's music chamber.

This went on for five years; and at last Gertrude and her husband slipped secretly out of Berlin. They got as far as Dresden, where they were detained by the Prussian Ambassador. Using all the general influence which she could command, Gertrude saved herself from the real danger that grew out of the King's displeasure; and after a while her contract was cancelled, and she was free, at the age of thirty-one, to make her way where she would throughout Europe— free, except for her husband.

First she tried Vienna, but unsuccessfully:

275

the young Emperor was fondest of light opera, in which Mara did badly. Then for a year or two she hovered generally about Austria and Germany, giving concerts and appearing occasionally in opera: it was at Munich, in 1780, that Mozart heard her sing, as mentioned above. Eventually she decided to go to Paris; and the pair made their way into France through Germany, Holland and Belgium, giving concerts in the larger towns, and carrying with them letters of introduction to Marie Antoinette.

v

It was in the year 1782—the year of Farinelli's death amid his pictures and harpsichords in the *palazzo* near Bologna—that Mara reached Paris. For four years the great singer in Paris there had been the Portuguese Luiza Rosa de Aguiar, known as Madame Todi from her marriage with Saverio Todi. This artist was peculiarly grateful to the French, but had failed consistently in Germany and in London: later on, however, she did well in most European countries.

Mara sang at the Concerts Spirituels, an old organization which was always open to the famous artists from foreign lands, and where she had been preceded by Farinelli, Caffarelli, Agujari, and hosts of others.

At once the war began. Those who were tired or jealous of Todi ranged themselves on the side of Mara; those whom Mara offended, or who had social dislike of anyone attached to the Mara faction, ranged themselves on the side of Todi. Conditions were not so disgraceful as those of the war in London fifty years earlier under the banners of Faustina and Cuzzoni, because neither Mara nor Todi was vigorously belligerent by nature; yet conditions were lively enough in a witty manner.

As the singers were equally good, the German excelling in bravura, the Portuguese in expression, absolute victory did not go to either of them :

> Todi by her melting voice
> With soft tears wets my eyes ;
> Brilliant Mara, filled with life,
> Wafts me astonished to the skies :
> One can ravish, the other enchant ;
> Yet chief pleasure always lies
> In the one that's singing now—

So wrote a minor poet, very fairly summing up the matter, and speaking for the sensible persons who were neither Todists nor Maradists.

VI

After a year or so, the two singers left Paris. Todi went to Russia, where for a time she was a person of power behind the throne, dangerous to courtiers and officials who offended her, or who offended the individuals she liked. In 1789 she was back in Paris; and then, in 1792, she settled quietly in Lisbon, with forty years of pleasant life before her, a husband, and eight children, the while Mara wandered restlessly over Europe, with many disastrous adventures and much financial distress.

Todi, when she died, left £15,000 in money and a still greater sum in jewels. . . . Writing in 1788, Dr. Burney says: "And as for Signora Todi, she must have improved very much since she was in England [1777], or we treated her very unworthily; for though her voice was thought to be feeble and seldom in tune while she was here, she had since been extremely admired in France, Spain, Russia and Germany, as a most touching and exquisite performer."

VII

Mara moved from Paris to London. It was in England that she was to be supremely successful, and it seems that, at the end of her life, it was her London experiences that remained most warmly in her remembrance.

She first appeared at some Pantheon Concerts. The Pantheon was a great place in Oxford Street, Poland Street, and Great Marlborough Street, built in 1770 for balls, masquerades, and music; the directors followed a most ambitious policy, and for a long time the Pantheon concerts seriously interfered with the opera: but the place

MARA

had a troublesome history, until some time in the middle of the nineteenth century it became the London offices of a firm of wine merchants, remaining so until this day.

Mara sang at six concerts, early in 1784; but there was a general election at the time, and she attracted no special notice. Later in the year, however (May 26th-29th and June 3rd-5th), came the first of the Handel Commemorations; she was chief singer here, and her victory was absolute; London raved about her, and the world was was at her feet. The audiences at Westminster Abbey numbered three thousand persons; and it is hardly too much to say that Mara alone of the singers and musicians made the Commemoration the success it was. This would be pleasant for the survivors of those men and women who, nearly twenty-five years before, had persuaded Johann Schmeling to make a singer of his child, not a violinist.

Except for visits to Italy, Mara remained mostly in England for eighteen years (1784-1802). Her work on the London opera stage began in 1786 in a pasticcio called *Didone abbandonata*. Operas of this kind were patchwork things, made of approved airs from other operas, which were fitted to new words suitable for the plot of the pasticcio, and usually selected by each singer for himself or herself. Thus if an artist had won fame in an aria at any time, that aria would be among those selected.

Mara's selections for *Didone* were :

(a)	*Son regina.*	Sacchini.
(b)	*Se il ciel mi divide.*	Piccini.
(c)	*Ah, non lasciarmi, nó.*	Mortellari.
(d)	a *Scena.*	Gazzaniga.

These pieces, as sung by Mara, made the production a success, because the majority of her
companions in the cast were not artists of first
order; the pieces were generally encored, the
Piccini piece invariably. (Piccini was the composer who was used in Paris to oppose the works
of Gluck.)

Didone was many times performed; and then,
the next year (1787) saw a revival of Handel's
Giulio Cesare. In this opera Cuzzoni (dead now
for seventeen years in Bologna, and some other
destitute old woman covering the buttons with
silk) had won supreme success. That was
sixty-three years before; but such was the new
interest in Handel that the revival was welcomed,
and Mara, singing the same part of Cleopatra,
gained added popularity.

It was only by her singing that she pleased;
she was a poor actress, of no figure, and, indeed,
not pleasant to look on, owing to her appearance
of weakness.

Her work in opera lasted up to 1791. She
then for eleven years turned exclusively to
oratorio and concerts, making plenty of money.
In 1802 she decided to leave England, and at her

farewell concert realized a profit of a thousand pounds.

Of course, she had enemies in London, and various other singers were put up against her; yet none was fine enough to weaken her position until her voice began to fade. And she was caricatured in the brutal manner which the gentlemen of the time thought permissible. In those days all the performers at a concert were accustomed to sit on the platform throughout the programme, coming forward to sing or play in turn. Mara could not do this, because the heat fatigued her; she made apologies, and fully explained matters: but her enemies still ridiculed her for what they chose to call pride, and they made delicate fun of her physical disabilities.

VIII

Here is the beginning of one of Cleopatra's songs in *Giulio Cesare*, with which Cuzzoni and Mara pleased people in the eighteenth century. Like scores of similar pieces in the forgotten Handel operas, it is beautiful music and should be revived by sopranos able to sing up to A. This song is of the expressive kind, not the *bravura*, though the original singers embellished slightly the written phrases. The accompaniment is for 'cello (the bass), viola, violin, and harpsichord, the latter following the 'cello and filling up chords according to the directions conveyed by the figures.

MAKERS OF MUSIC

Non disperar, non dis-perar chi sa se al

Regno non av-rai, av-rai forte in a - mor . .

(VIOLIN.)

se al

TODI AND MARA

Regno non avrai, Av-rai for-te in a-mor, av-
rai forte in a-mor chi sa, chi sa.

IX

When Gertrude Mara left London in 1802,
she had little money, for what she received she
spent—or her lover for the time being spent.
The last of these was a young flautist named
Florio.

Although the power, beauty and brilliance of
her voice was gone, she had to enter on a lengthy
concert tour.   Paris was reached for the last time

in 1806; but at that time the singer Grassini was there (I shall speak of Grassini in a moment), and by contrast Mara was as much a tale that is told as was the recollection of the Todists and the Maradists.

Mara now was fifty-seven; she realized that her life of public singing was over, and that nothing remained but the life of a teacher. She was without money, and decided that Moscow offered the best scope for pupils.

And so to Moscow she went, travelling the long miles from Paris into the heart of Russia. She did well enough. Gradually she accumulated a few possessions, and knew some slight ease of mind. But Napoleon, and the fate which followed this singer, destroyed both her ease of mind and her material possessions.

We read of the burning of Moscow as a more or less abstract point in history, or as a glorious deed of national sacrifice. Reflecting on Gertrude Mara, we can read of it as an event that terribly disturbed thousands of persons. She was ruined by the fire. All she owned was burned, except what she wore or could carry; and in the dead of winter the old woman had to scramble into a waggon, with a crowd of other agitated persons, and find a home somewhere else.

She went to the seaport town of Reval, where about a third of the population were German. Here she was well received, for her fame was great; and here she was soon busy again with pupils.

The story is rather obscure; but it seems fairly certain that in 1819, when she was in her seventieth year, restlessness seized her and an emotional desire to visit London once more. To London therefore she came, from her home on the shores of the Gulf of Finland, to sing yet again in public, and to look up what former friends remained, from 1802, from 1784, or from 1760. Perhaps she saw Miss Burney, or Master Barron, or Master Cervetto; none older could be alive from that remote year of her debut as a violinist.

One thing is certain; her concert was a complete failure. So she made her way north again to Reval, there to live another thirteen years, until she died in 1833, eight months before Todi (blind now for several years) died in Lisbon.

A new world existed when she died. Beethoven, born ten years after she played violin in London, had finished his work; and she was become entirely historical. A book dealing with her life up to 1792 had been written and published in 1823 by G. G. Grosheim; her story had also been told in full in J. F. Rochlitz's *Für Freunde der Tonkunst* (1824-1832): and old Goethe, acquainted with the youthful Mendelssohn, had sent a poem to her in 1831. The eighteenth century in which she began was ended; it all lay on the other side of the Revolution ; and

285

with Mara ended the line of the eighteenth-century singers.

But the nineteenth century was already crowded with *its* masters of singing, and men and women of equal ability, and of even superior fame, were active in the musical countries of Europe.

XXV. BANTI, GRASSINI,
AND AUDIENCES

NEARLY all the great singers of the eighteenth
century were good musicians and hard workers.
They laboured for years at the business of correctly producing and placing the voice—or, as
it was then called, *directing* it, and would often
work for from five to ten years at the elements
of technique. They had to be good musicians,
because in those days a singer was expected to
vary, expand, and develop the melody written
by the composer; they had to add trills, runs,
"divisions," and other decorations, all of which
demanded true knowledge of the science of music.
A singer was condemned if he or she showed
bad taste in the embellishments.

These men and women had for the most part
good voices by nature, else they would never
have been great singers; but they brought as
much art to their work, and deserve credit as
fully as nature herself. For all their pride and
foolishness, they were true artists according to the
understanding of the age.

I

One singer, however, of the latter half of the
eighteenth century, who won enormous fame,
was neither a good worker nor an educated
musician, but a lazy person blessed with that
kind of ability which the birds have. This was

Brigitta Giorgi, a Viennese: she married a dancer named Banti, and is generally spoken of in history by her married name.

Brigitta's father was a gondolier, and so by custom he had the right of free admission to the theatres. She sang in the streets, until the notice of a well-to-do music-lover was drawn to her, when she was enabled to take a few lessons; the outcome of which was little more than the discovery that she was a really gifted singer.

In 1778, being then nineteen years old, and with nothing to lose by the way, she journeyed to Paris, walking, begging a lift in a cart, and singing at cafés and public places for means of subsistence.

Arrived in Paris, she secured engagements to sing in the cafés, until one evening a director of the opera heard her. This man arranged an interview. He found she knew nothing of music, but that after hearing a song two or three times she could render it perfectly. Her voice having a truly wonderful beauty, and her instinctive musicianship being perfect, he gave her a chance to appear in public.

Brigitta sang a song in the interval between two acts of a Gluck opera (such interludes were the customary thing in those days), and Paris was enraptured. Her engagement was confirmed, and she sang regularly.

But she was careless, absent-minded, and thoroughly unwilling to study. Let them play or sing a song to her, and explain its meaning and character, and she would give it in a manner not to be approached by anyone else. Indeed, she would invest it with an undreamed-of beauty and significance. But no more. And when she once started upon the song, she would keep it up for half-an-hour. The *da capo* aria is in the form A B A; the second A is an exact repeat of the first, and the B leads directly into it: thus you can go on infinitely, making A B A B A B A as long as time lasts. Brigitta, revelling in the sensuous loveliness of sound, in the exquisite ease of her production, and in the abandonment of mood, would continue the circle until someone told her she had better stop, so that the rest of the entertainment might continue: the audience, revelling in the same, were equally happy with her in this infinite progression.

Her fame reached England, and in 1779 or 1780 she was engaged to sing at the Pantheon concerts. The management paid her a good salary, but stipulated that a hundred pounds of this should be expended on musical instruction. Various great teachers took her in hand. They tried hard, and some were patient; yet all failed.

The fact was, that Brigitta did not want to learn. Without effort she could sing and act, both in grand opera and in comic; and this being so, what need to trouble farther? She could not sing " from notes," and it was a trouble for her to pick out a tune from the score; but she

could always command help, and did not intend
to make life miserable by hard work.

Up to 1802 she sang in England and on the
Continent; and then, in 1806, she died at
Bologna, aged forty-seven, leaving her husband
with one daughter.   Banti bequeathed her larynx
to the museum at Bologna, where it was preserved
in spirits.

II

Banti and Mara, when they left England in
1802, left the field to Mrs. Billington, who
between 1801 and 1811 was the most sought-
after singer in this country.   She was the daughter
of a Saxon musician who had lived the greater
part of his life in London, and we generally look
on her as an Englishwoman.   Her husband was a
double-bass player named James Billington.
There had been something of a contest between
Mara and Mrs. Billington in the last years of the
century, but Banti and Mrs. Billington were on
good terms—at least towards the end of Banti's
life here.

In 1794, when this singer was twenty-six
years old, she sang in the opera at Naples: one
evening, just as she and her husband were setting
out for the theatre, he was struck down by
apoplexy, dying almost in a moment; a little
later, Mount Vesuvius burst out in eruption;
the Neapolitans put these two events together,

and came to the conclusion that they represented God's anger that a heretic should be allowed to sing in the town—there was almost a riot, and Mrs. Billington was actually in danger for a time; but things quietened down, and she was allowed to complete her engagement.

III

Mrs. Billington seems to have been more singer than actor; but Josephina Grassini (1773-1850) was, in the opinion of some writers of the time, an actress equal to Mrs. Siddons. . . . All we write or say of former singers and instrumentalists and actors is at second or third hand; by imaginative thought and sympathy we may be able to create them afresh in our own minds, yet the moment we put pen to paper that fabricated impression fades, and the subject again becomes an abstraction. Even when we set out to describe performers of our own time, and to convey in words the feelings they have aroused in us, the most vivid impressions will refuse to submit to the operation of verbal statement. In all my reading of contemporary writers, I have met with no remarks on these Mara's, Faustina's, and the rest, but such as resolve themselves into a string of common adjectives. Thus I am acquainted with nothing worthy a literal quotation.

But now, arriving at this singer, Josephina

MAKERS OF MUSIC

Grassini, I am reminded of a passage by De Quincey which certainly lives; and in order to bring a breath of reality into these pages I will copy the passage in full. A little later on, I shall copy a lively operatic criticism from a source not likely to be familiar to my young readers. These two extracts are animated by genuine feeling, the one recollective in the manner of art, the other immediate in the way of journalism.

You know of Thomas De Quincey, without doubt—that strange compound of genius and commonplace talent, who might have been one of our great masters of literature, but just missed his aim. He will become a living figure for you as you study the period of Wordsworth and Coleridge, and one day you are sure to read with eagerness his *Confessions of an English Opium-eater*, from which I take these next lines.

" . . . I used to fix beforehand how often within a given time, when, and with what accessory circumstances of festal joy, I would commit a debauch of opium . . . once in three weeks sufficed; and the time selected was either a Tuesday or a Saturday night; my reason for which was this: Tuesday and Saturday were for many years the regular nights of performance at the King's Theatre (or Opera House); and there it was in those times [1804-1806] that Grassini sang; and her voice (the richest of

GRASSINI

contraltos) was delightful to me beyond all that
I had ever heard. Yes; or have since heard; or
ever shall hear. I know not what may be the
state of the opera-house now, having never been
within its walls for seven or eight years; but at
that time it was by much the most pleasant place
of resort in London for passing an evening.
Half-a-guinea admitted you to the pit, under
the troublesome condition, however, of being
en grande tenue [that is, in full evening dress].
But to the gallery five shillings admitted you;
and that gallery was subject to far less annoyance
than the pit of most theatres. The orchestra
was distinguished by its sweet and melodious
grandeur from all English orchestras; the composition of which, I confess, is not acceptable to
my ear, from the predominance of the clangorous
instruments, and in some instances from the
tyranny of the violin. Thrilling was the pleasure
with which almost always I heard this angelic
Grassini. Shivering with expectation I sat,
when the time drew near for her golden epiphany;
shivering I rose from my seat, incapable of rest,
when that heavenly and harp-like voice sang its
own victorious welcome in its prelusive *threttánelo-
threttánelo* [the echoic words used by Aristophanes
to express the sound of a musical instrument].
The choruses were divine to hear; and, when
Grassini appeared in some interlude, as she
often did, and poured forth her passionate soul
as Andromache at the tomb of Hector, etc., I

question whether any Turk, of all that ever entered the paradise of opium-eaters, can have had half the pleasure I had. . . . All this was to be had for five shillings, that being the price of admission to the gallery; or, if a man preferred the high-bred society of the pit, even this might be had for half-a-guinea; or, in fact, for half-a-crown less, by purchasing beforehand a ticket at the music shops. And, over and above the music of the stage and the orchestra, I had all around me, in the intervals of the performance, the music of the Italian language talked by Italian women, for the gallery was usually crowded with Italians; and I listened with a pleasure such as that with which Weld, the traveller, lay and listened, in Canada, to the sweet laughter of Indian women; for, the less you understand of a language, the more sensible you are to the melody or harshness of its sounds. . . ."

The expression " harp-like," applied by De Quincey to the voice of this singer, may seem strange ; but it is natural enough: the executive and tonal qualities of a singer like Grassini would be pure and facile as the tones of such an instrument.

Grassini sang her own " victorious welcome " in a " prelusive " passage. This was a custom of the time. Singers, before the music of the piece began, could in certain conditions entertain themselves and their audiences by giving a long brilliant warble. Instrumentalists could do the

CORA

GRASSINI AS CORA

in

THE VIRGIN OF THE SUN

same with a brilliant prelude ; pianists, indeed, not only preludized to a piece, but actually " codaised " it, continuing, as long as inspiration lasted, a lively improvisation. Concert manners and methods were formerly quite different from to-day.

IV

The Italians among whom De Quincey sat were quiet in the manner which is conventionally, but incorrectly, held to be characteristic of English people.

In Italy for many years they had been noisy. The audiences there had no interest in the drama of an opera; that is, they did not care to follow the piece intellectually, and except in the great emotional arias they played cards, ate food or drank wine, chatted freely, stood up and called out to friends on the opposite side of the theatre, and entertained themselves generally. When a favourite singer came on the stage, they rose and yelled approval; and if the number first sung was not of importance, they kept up their yelling all through its performance. Profound silence fell upon an impassioned song: then, at its close, the tumult began again; gentlemen beat sticks against the benches, and people in the topmost seats flung into the body of the theatre printed copies of a poem lauding the actor who had just performed. The yelling went on until the

295

piece or the entire scene was repeated. The performance, beginning about eight, would end about half-past twelve; if an important person in the audience wanted to get away early, yet desired to see the last act, this would be put on before the act preceding it, and so after hero and heroine died, hero and heroine would come to life again and resume their interrupted troubles. . . . Writing from Italy in May, 1831, Mendelssohn says that the orchestra and chorus of an opera were poor, and that "the first violinist, all through the opera, beats the four quarters of each bar on a tin candlestick, which is often more distinctly heard than the voices (it sounds somewhat like *obbligato* castanets, only louder); and yet in spite of this the instruments and voices are never together. Every little instrumental solo is adorned with old-fashioned flourishes, and bad taste pervades the whole performance, which is totally devoid of genius, fire, and spirit."

In England the people used to manage the management of a theatre, and if a favourite singer was dismissed or not engaged they would make a disturbance and refuse to let the performance be carried out. The most famous of these "rows" was that which took place in Her Majesty's Theatre in 1840, which was caused by M. Laporte not having engaged the singer Tamburini. Our English approval never developed to the stage told of on page 352, where

AUDIENCES

I quote a passage descriptive of Clara Novello's successes in Rome; nor did we ever have a riot at all like those the Italians sometimes had, though, (as intimated in the footnote on page 356) we could interrupt proceedings by noise.

At Saragossa the theatre was the scene of a serious *emeute* between the partisans of two rival actresses, Senoras Campos and Roca. Bottles, apples, sticks, etc., flew about in all directions. The Infante and Princess Carlota precipitately left the theatre, and the Alcalde, after vainly trying to appease the combatants, called in a detachment of soldiers, who, after a liberal distribution of knocks with the butts of their muskets, succeeded in clearing the place.

I copy this paragraph from *The Pictorial Times* for March 18th, 1843. Nor did our " floral tributes " ever become so lavish as those of the Italians. Consider the significance of the following piece of news, which I take from *The Pictorial Times* of April 29th, the same year (Cerito and Taglioni were dancers, but singers were similarly favoured) :

The last appearance of Cerito in Milan was marked by an enthusiasm, fortunately—we may perhaps say—unknown in this country. She was called upon the stage 52 times, and

297

1,494 bouquets and 836 garlands were thrown to her. Among the bouquets was one of such gigantic proportions that it required two porters to carry it to the theatre. [Surely this was not one of those *thrown* to the dancer !] It is expected by the Taglioni-ites that the approaching reception of their favourite will be still more pompous, nearly all the hot-houses and flower gardens of Lombardy having been bought up for the occasion.

No contemporary fame was ever wider and more
assured than that of John Braham—not Caruso's,
or that of Sims Reeves. For nearly fifty years
he reigned as the King of Tenors, and it seems
he held his position justifiably, though not a man
who lived and worked for the higher art. Visitors
from the Continent—among them the great
Italian singers themselves—used to exclaim with
surprise at his singing, and say that in the whole
of Italy there was no tenor like him. He is
known to us chiefly to-day as the composer of
the song called *The Death of Nelson* ; few young
students of music are aware that he was the first
Sir Huon in Weber's opera of *Oberon* (1826), or
that he wrote more songs and duets than any
other musician of his period.

He was for many years a sort of landmark,
and writers of a later period referred to him as an
institution. Such reference is not infrequently
made to well-known actors and musicians. Albert
Smith, for example, in his " Christopher
Tadpole " (Chapter 5), allows his contemporaries
John Parry and Miss Dolby to enter the scene
and walk about and smile for a moment. Albert
Smith, however, was himself an entertainer, and
his action does not count for much. But the fame
of Braham is shown forcefully by Thackeray,
who in the first chapter of " The Newcomes,"
when outlining the necessary delights of London
youth in his younger days, includes going to
Drury Lane to see Braham in *Fra Diavolo*.

Thackeray's book dates from 1854. Auber's opera was produced in London in 1831. Braham was still alive in 1854, though perhaps Thackeray did not know the fact.

Braham became a wealthy man; his fees were princely, as when about the age of thirty he could command £2,100 for singing on fifteen nights in a town like Dublin: but when he was drawing near sixty years of age he lost his money—to the tune of fifty or sixty thousand pounds—in some theatrical speculations, and had to take to the road again.

I

He had started life very poor. His parents, Abraham by name, died young. Poverty was their portion, and their son was left destitute. The story is that he had to look after himself, making some sort of living by selling pens, pencils, and the like, in the streets.

John Braham was born in 1774; in 1787 he attracted by some means the notice of a famous Jewish singer of the time named Leoni, who took him in hand musically, and perhaps made it unnecessary for the boy (now thirteen) to wander the streets of London peddling writing materials.

Almost immediately John was fit to sing in public: he was engaged to provide some of the entertainments which came between the acts of

JOHN BRAHAM

operas or after plays and farces and ballets, and he sailed into the first period of his fame on a song called " The Soldier, Tired of War's Alarms."*

This kind of work went on until his voice broke. He was now in difficulties again ; Leoni disappeared, though another friend was found in a man named Abraham Goldschmidt, and having mastered piano playing, Braham supported himself by teaching that art until his man's voice developed. Then he started singing again; and had the good fortune to find a friend in an Italian musician of Bath, named Rauzzini, at one of whose concerts Braham sang in 1794. Rauzzini gave him lessons for some time, until the young man was fit to sing in the lighter kind of London opera.

For two or three years he did well, in opera, in oratorio, and at concerts. He then went to Paris and Italy, singing with Nancy Storace, and generally having a profitable time. His repute in Italy indeed, was so excellent that for a while

*After this book was in print, I came across a work by the son of Henry Russell entitled " Representative Actors." The author, W. Clark Russell, elder brother of Sir Landon Ronald, and famous for his novels of the sea, gathers into this book some hundreds of contemporary criticisms and records of British actors and opera singers from the sixteenth century to the middle of the nineteenth century. From one of the notices of Braham, written in 1831, I see that when " Master Braham " made his first appearance in 1787 " he was very little noticed, and attracted no attention for years after. . . . He must have been about fourteen, and small for his age."

he was a serious trouble to the famous Mrs. Billington, who was then in that country; but these two were eventually reconciled, and became friends.

John Braham, now as in the later years of his life, wanted to be looked on more as composer than singer; and he had certainly determined that he would make money out of songs: he therefore attended seriously to the study of vocal composition, and for some months studied under a musician in Milan, at the cost of many engagements in other towns that would have brought in handsome fees.

We smile over his songs nowadays; but we should remember that he took them seriously enough, and that he put himself out to acquire a technique of song-composition in a period when he might have had a lively and profitable time singing.

II

When twenty-seven years old, Braham came back to England. This was in 1801. He at once leapt into the foremost place among the great singers of the time; and his position so steadily maintained itself that his art became traditional—he seemed an immortal, and though his final appearance was not made until fifty-one years later (1852), it was not felt that age had

BRAHAM

done much more harm than a lowering of his range.

The "operas" in which he appeared are numbered by the dozen, and for all of them he was accustomed to write his own songs. Their character can be seen by a few titles: *The Cabinet ; The English Fleet ; Thirty Thousand ; Out of Place ; Family Quarrels ; The Paragraph ; Kais* (or "Love in the Desert "); *The Americans ; The Devil's Bridge ;* and *False Alarms.* It was in *The Americans* that the song appeared of the death of Nelson, the year being 1811.

His song of *Aileen Aroon* sold nearly a quarter of a million copies : *All's Well; The King, God Bless Him !,* and scores of others, sold well for a half-century, and are still to be met with in shilling collections of popular songs. (And they are still to be heard in country places. I myself a little while ago heard two old men sing at a "free and easy " the duet *All's Well,* which had been their standing item in the village for more than fifty years, and the robust seriousness with which the old boys did their piece was delightful: the junior of the pair, a youthful person who had not yet struck eighty, gave at the same meeting Henry Russell's *A Life on the Ocean Wave.*)

Here is the first phrase of a Braham song. Being published for the use of amateurs, the decorations generally added extemporaneously by the singer were written out by the composer and printed. The quotation, therefore, illustrates

303   U

first the compositions of John Braham, and, secondly, that manner of embellishing melody which is so constantly spoken of in musical history.*

1st Verse — Oh, ve - ry sweet was

2nd Verse — This blow - ing rose re -

3rd Verse — And oh! these dew - y

morn - ing's dawn to me, to

sem - bles thee, My mo - - dest,

gems I prize, They sparkle, they

*The following shows how regularly Braham sang his own songs. It is a list of the pieces he gave at the Birmingham Musical Festivals between 1817 and 1826. Many oratorios were included in the "schemes" (the programmes), and also many songs by other composers.

1817. *Echo Duet* (with Mrs. Salmon. *The Bewildered Maid.* (Duet) *When thy bosom heaves the sigh. Is there a heart that never loved? Nelson.*

1820. Braham did not sing in the Festival this year.

1823. Another *Echo Duet. The Soldier's Love-Letter.* And a piece by his old friend of Bath, Rauzzini, entitled *Alfred in the Neat-herd's Cot.*

1826. The *Echo Duet* of 1817.

JOHN BRAHAM

me,   my   Ma - ry,   When

mo - dest   Ma - ry: For

spar - - kle,   Ma - ry: So
[forte]   [piano]

thou   and   I   stray'd   o'er   the

in . . . its   leaves   I   think   I

like . . . . the di - monds in   thine
[forte, with energy]

lawn to - ge-ther, to-ge - ther, Ma - ry.   &c.

see   thy blushes, thy blushes,   Ma - ry!   &c.

eyes,   My love-ly,   love-ly   Ma - ry.   &c.

305

MAKERS OF MUSIC

Braham was a " primitive " singer. He sang
with a magnificent energy, with enormous force,
vehement passion, and irresistible conviction.
His intonation was perfect, and he could fly up
and down the chromatic scale in an unheard-of
manner, his notes as true as his velocity was
amazing. Singers of one kind concentrate their
qualities of strength, zeal, and feeling, and
become forcible by a fine intellectual command;
this is the dignity of art, akin to that dignity
which marks composers like Bach, and it is
found in such singers as John Coates and the
late Gervase Elwes: these men have ample power
at command, and when they loose out into
dramatic passion, the effect is most moving.
Singers of the other kind—that is, of the type
Braham represented to perfection, constantly
overwhelm our intellectual senses, appealing
without reserve to the emotional. They never
spare themselves, and live in a world of exciteo
furore. It is always the simple emotions they
stir; they are not reflective, but bold and vivid:
yet when as musicianly and as gifted vocally as
Braham, they can sing well in the quieter lyrica
parts of opera; and their delivery of *recitative*
is often perfect.

We gather from the records of the time
that Braham both sang and shouted, but that
even his shouts were true to the musical scale.

JOHN BRAHAM

He was wise enough in this direction, and generally reserved such effects for the shilling gallery at Drury Lane or for provincial theatres. Sometimes he made a mistake, as once at a festival (either at Bath or Gloucester), where in the first day of the meeting he was hissed off the platform; but he at once realized his mistake, and was not offended by the treatment.

Thus at the festival just mentioned, he immediately went to a music-lover of the place and asked him what the event might be taken to signify, for he had never before been so rebuffed. The gentleman answered :

" To tell you the truth, sir, if you wish to be heard and esteemed here, you must sing."

Braham accepted the rebuke and the implied criticism. He merely answered :

" I understand you, sir."

And the next day, when he had to take part in a performance of the Messiah, he showed the people that he could indeed sing.

The critics objected to his variety of styles, for he would to one audience sing a Handel song in the manner of a great and true artist, and the next day sing the same piece to another audience in the manner of a charlatan ; and all for the immediate profit of giving them pleasure. A friend once told him that the critics were justified in their attitude towards him, since this extreme variability reacted for the bad on his best manner.

Said Braham : " Do you mean to say that if my practice had been less multifarious I should be a better singer to-day ? "

The friend said " Yes."

Braham thought for a few moments, and then said : " I never had an audience able to appreciate me. Give me such an audience, and then see how I will sing ! "

Braham had his unfilled ambition, and knew what it was to desire purity in art.

An enormous vigour, as sure and certain as it was vital, seems to have marked everything Braham did. His singing of Purcell's *Come, if you dare, our trumpets sound*, used to electrify people, because in it was all that simple and unstudied passion which, passing into his songs, made them a precious possession for his generation. And his singing of Handel's *Deeper and deeper still* used to move people to tears. Observe how he affected even persons like Lamb, who was generally bored by music :

Do you like Braham's singing ? The little Jew has bewitched me. I follow him like as the boys followed Tom the Piper. He cures me of melancholy as David cured Saul; but I don't throw stones at him as Saul did at David in payment. I was insensible to music till he gave me a new sense. O that you could go to the new opera of *Kais* to-night ! 'Tis all about Eastern manners; it would just suit

JOHN BRAHAM

you. It describes the wild Arabs, wandering
Egyptians, lying dervishes, and all that sort
of people, to a hair. You needn't ha' gone
so far to see what you see, if you saw it as I do
every night at Drury Lane Theatre. Braham's
singing, when it is impassioned, is finer than
Mrs. Siddons's or Mr. Kemble's acting !
And when it is not impassioned, it is as good
as hearing a person of fine sense talking.
[Lamb probably refers here to his delivery
of *recitative*, and incidentally gives a perfect
description of that art.] The brave little
Jew !

(Letter to Thomas Manning, 26 Feb., 1808.)

Sir Walter Scott, another man without the
musical mind or ear, said that Braham was a
beast of an actor, though an angel of a singer.

It would be his wonderful use of the falsetto
voice that touched people like Scott and Lamb.
He was the first English singer to master this
department of singing. Formerly our tenors
managed it badly. Their transition from the
natural voice to the falsetto was so abrupt as to be
laughable, and one of them, a singer named
Johnstone, though his falsetto in itself was good,
managed the change so badly that he was called
Signor Bubble and Squeak. Braham, on the
other hand, took the falsetto in such a manner
that no one could tell the exact point of transition.
He would glide slowly or quickly by semitones

309

over his entire range, and by making the change
now on one note and now on another would
confuse the most experienced listener.

IV

In a letter written by Weber to his wife are
several remarks about Braham. As this letter
does not seem to be well known, I quote from it
here, the more willingly in that it gives us a
general insight into the production of *Oberon*,
The year is 1826.

> Miss Paton is a singer of the first rank,
> and will play Reiza divinely. Braham not
> less so, though in a totally different style.
> There are also several good tenors; and I
> really cannot see why the English singing
> should be so much abused. The singers have
> a perfectly good Italian education, fine voices
> and expression. The orchestra is not remark-
> able, but still very good, and the choruses
> particularly so. In short, I feel quite at ease
> as to the fate of Oberon. . . . Braham begs
> for a grand scena instead of his first air, which,
> in fact, was not written for him, and is rather
> high. The thought of it was at first quite
> horrible; I could not hear of it. At last I
> promised, when the opera was completed,
> it should be done if I had time enough; and

now the writing of this grand scena, a con-
founded battle-piece and what not, is lying
before me, and I am about to set to work, yet
with the greatest reluctance. But what can
I do ? Braham knows his public, and is
idolized by them. For Germany, however,
I shall keep the opera as it is. I hate by
anticipation the air I am going to compose
(to-day, I hope). Adieu, and now for the
battle ! . . . So the battle is over—that is
to say, the half of the scene. To-morrow
shall the Turks roar, the French shout for joy,
and the warriors cry out " Victory ! "

The " battle-picture " is a grand scena, and
an aria beginning, " Yes, even Love to Fame
must yield." The piece for which it was substituted is the air " From Boyhood trained in
Battle-field." The latter is always sung in
Germany; Weber did not care for the new piece,
even after it was finished, and it is of inferior
quality. Braham liked it, and sang it about the
country a good deal. But another piece which
Weber composed for Braham—the prayer " Ruler
of this awful Hour "—is one of the loveliest
passages of the work: Weber wrote this happily,
not unhappily as in the case of the scena; and it
is retained in the German performances of
Oberon.

MAKERS OF MUSIC

V

Having lost his money by the year 1836, John Braham set manfully to work again. In a little while he accumulated a small sum, and he then (with one of his sons) ventured on a long tour in America. This, according to one report, was financially successful; according to another, it was unsuccessful.

Returning to England in 1843, now in his seventieth year, this stalwart singer—who, be it remembered, was a tenor—continued his public work. He gave concerts in London and at various places in the country, and kept up this work for several years, his last notes of all sounding at a London concert in the March of 1852. Thus he was a public singer for sixty-five years: it is no wonder that he became a tradition and seemed an immortal, for old men at his last concert were unborn when he first appeared.

Let us read a report of the first concert given on his return from America. I copy the following from the *Dramatic and Musical Review* for February 18th, 1843, a poor sort of periodical run by two brothers of the name of Eames, who particularly hated J. W. Davison, at that time editor of another paper called the *Musical Examiner*.

We had just time in our last number to congratulate the public upon the reappearance ot the veteran Braham, in robust health, and with voice decidedly less impaired than just previous to his quitting the shores of Old England. His welcome, from a very full house, was such as might have been expected; warm, enthusiastic and hearty. In the first song, " The last words of Marmion," he had not brought himself completely into play ; but in " William Tell," which followed, and in all his succeeding songs, he evinced that firm and vigorous grasp of his subject—that extraordinary volume and flexibility of voice, that reminded us of former days. He transposed " Deeper and deeper still," from the key of G to F ; but he gave it with great effect, notwithstanding the presence of those embellishments which we have always considered blemishes in this kind of music. He was encored in a pretty little ballad of Knight's called " The Miniature," in S. Lover's " Molly Bawn," and in " Scots wha hae "; the latter of which (songs) he acted without accompaniment. [Can you not see the old man tearing out this Scotch tune, singing alone without the pianoforte ?] " The Death of Nelson " created quite a sensation. Mr. Charles Braham, who made his debut in England, has a sound, even, tenor voice, of good natural compass, and considerable power; he was not always strictly in tune, but this may more properly be attributed to the nervousness of a first appearance than to a defective ear. He is very young, and we believe has not sung in public much more than a year; but we have no hesitation in saying that he has it in his power to become a first-rate tenor singer; he sang Rooke's beautiful song, " My Boyhood's Home," and was encored in " There's a Charm in Spring " (a weak composition, from the Village Coquettes), as well as in the duets with his father, " Gallop on gaily " and " All's Well." Mr. Braham presided at the pianoforte throughout the evening. A second entertainment is given on Thursday of this week, when the selection will doubtless be of a less popular description.

The old man must indeed have been " in robust health," for his country tour in 1843 embraced concerts in the Channel Islands— with an adventure which is thus told in the *Morning Post* for one of the days in August :

Mr. Braham's career was, a few days since, nearly brought to a close by the rash attempt to cross, with his son Charles and his friend Mr. Torre, in a small open boat, from Guernsey to Jersey—the difficult and dangerous navigation in that quarter being unknown to any of the party, all of whom were given up for lost by their friends in the former island, on hearing of their temerity. After having been

MADAME VESTRIS

"rocked in the cradle of the deep" for upwards of fifteen hours, and exposed during the whole night to a rough sea, they providentially reached terra firma in safety, drenched, and famished; but the veteran was none the worse for his perilous adventure, during which the patience and fortitude he displayed are said to have been exemplary.

Here was no small adventure for any man, to spend fifteen hours in a small open boat. without food or sleep, in a rough sea that washed constantly over the vessel, no sailor present, and the night to be struggled through; but for a man in his seventieth year it was truly perilous. However, John Braham survived, and probably joked of the experience to the day of his death, which took place on February 17th, 1856.

He survives to-day by his song, "The Death of Nelson," but more intimately and profitably he survives by the lesson he affords of pluck, activity, generous use of his musical gifts, and sincere work in the particular line of music which was laid down for him.

.   .   .   .   .   .

Other singers beside Braham preferred the lighter lyric drama to the more advanced Italian opera, and made themselves famous and well-to-do by the singing of songs rather than of elaborate arias.

Among them was Madame Vestris, of whom

is a beautiful water-colour drawing by Alfred Chalon in the National Portrait Gallery. This picture gives Madame Vestris in the part of Fatima, in Weber's *Oberon* (for she took part with Braham in the production of *Oberon*), and it shows us what a lovely woman she was.

Her grandfather was the engraver Bartolozzi, and her maiden name was Lucia Elizabeth Bartolozzi. When sixteen years old (she was born, apparently in London, in 1797) she married a ballet-dancer named Vestris, who deserted her two or three years later, himself dying in 1825.

Her voice was of that lusciously rich contralto, easy, natural, and voluptuous, which inevitably makes a singer popular when allied with ability to act and beauty of face and figure. She could have won and held a foremost place in Italian opera; but there was a delightful indolence in her nature that made her prefer the easier work in such things as *The Haunted Tower*, *Paul Pry*, and the like.

We think of Braham always in connection with *The Death of Nelson*; similarly in the case of Madame Vestris we think of her in connection with C. E. Horn's *Cherry Ripe*, which she introduced into Poole's *Paul Pry* in 1825. Another song that people crowded to hear her sing was *Meet me by moonlight alone*.

In 1838 " Eliza Lucy," as she then was named, married Charles James Matthews, with whom

MADAME VESTRIS

she carried on some theatrical speculations.
The year of her death was 1856. . . . Young
romanticists, wishing a charming heroine for a
musical story, could safely make use of this
singer.

XXVII. CATALANI, PASTA, THE GARCIAS, AND ALBERTAZZI

I

IT is not easy to make up one's mind about such a person as Angelica Catalani, who during the first quarter of the nineteenth century was supreme among soprano singers.

She was a ruinously expensive artist, being avaricious of money; yet during the period of her fame she frequently gave her services in the cause of charity, whereby in all some three-quarters of a million pounds were secured, and at the end of her life she gave lessons, without charge, to poor girls of ability.

She was extraordinarily proud, jealous, and self-sufficient, so that she would suffer no rival, nor indeed allow another gifted singer to appear on the stage with her in a suitable part and she strove constantly to be the one eminent individual, not only in a theatre, but in a town, making use of any means to effect her end; yet she never sang without kneeling down and praying fervently for God's blessing on her labours.*

She did not care to perform slow, expressive, pathetic music; yet in an air like " I know that my Redeemer liveth " she could thrill listeners to their very marrow.

*This last, however, could easily enough be explained, though at the risk of offending people, and at the cost of a long exposition of a certain type of the sentimentally religious temperament.

From the Ceci collection

VESTRIS

CATALANI

Her tastes in music were "vicious," and she had no emotional warmth; yet she was as fine on the stage in the grand and imposing parts as she was delightful in light parts like that of Susanna in Mozart's *Marriage of Figaro*.

She was full of mannerisms—for example, in singing a shake she wobbled her jaw in the ugliest way ; yet for thirty years she was an idol of the musical world, the members of which forgot her peculiarities in the fullness, power, and beauty of her voice.

She had a husband who was really a detestable man; yet she seemed to have loved him, and to have been happy with him, "after her fashion."

Altogether Angelica Catalani was a mixture. But the sum total of the impressions received in reading and thinking about her is an abiding idea of someone not to be liked or admired.

She was an Italian, born in 1779. For three years her general education was carried on in a convent, where she sang in the services and proved a very profitable member of the establishment: people used to crowd the chapel to hear the sensational child-singer, and their gifts (or the charges made for seats) were proportionate to the excitement she caused. But the heads of the convent did not trouble to teach her music correctly, or to look after the technical side of her art; and it was in these days that the girl acquired her mannerisms of execution and her bad taste in art. When later in life some older

319   x

singers with whom she acted tried to teach her, they seem to have found her unable to understand what they were driving at.

Leaving the convent, Angelica sang in opera in various Italian towns. For a time she sang in the expressive manner that was then desired, as in the music of the Mozart school; but here she was not successful, because her nature was not in sympathy with the style. And so she turned to that *bravura* manner which was her particular gift, to win almost immediately an astonishing fame. The enthusiasm of the public was wild in character, and " the Catalani " knew that fortune was hers; which made her happy. She was at this time only sixteen.

In 1804 she went to Lisbon, at a salary of £3,000 a year. There she married a man named Valebrique, a Burgundian, who (I believe) died in 1828, twenty-one years before Angelica. He was a soldier person, stupid, ignorant, extravagant, fond of gambling and unlucky at the sport, money-grasping, greedy, and so on. This gentleman determined to work his wife's gifts and fame for all they were worth; and for more than twenty years he and she exploited her art in the most shameless fashion, for money.

There has never been, in the whole course of musical history, such a story to be told, apart from this of Angelica Catalani. It is not a pleasant story, and there is no need to detail it here

CATALANI

Catalani and M. de Valebrique came to London in 1806. Mrs. Billington was just retired, and Grassini ("gorged with English gold," as De Quincey puts it) had gone off to Paris, there to please Napoleon and to be taught by him to hate the English. Thus Catalani started in England with no serious rival.

In her first year here she earned £16,700, all of which of course came from the pockets of the worshipping public. They gave her £2,000 to sing at a festival; and "God Save the King," with "Rule Britannia," were delivered aloud by her to the under-counterpoint of two hundred pounds.

How the patriotism of the audience must have thrilled to know that the British Empire was wealthy enough to have its National Anthem sung at 17s. 6d. a syllable (or, if only one verse was rendered, £2 12s. 6d.). Our greatness was never more indubitably displayed, nor by finer means; and incidentally, by the same process we supported the Art of Music and Song.

It must, of course, have been a wonderful experience to hear Catalani sing these songs. Her voice was glorious in purity and force, she declaimed with a wonderful energy, and the strongest band of the time was little more than as a mandoline by comparison. Men of that time who lived on into the Wagnerian epoch said that she would have dominated, almost equally, the great orchestra of Wagner, with its heavy brass. And she had entire control of this great voice, so that she could give the same passage as perfectly in the softest tone as in the loudest.

Fo six or seven years she was despotic in England, making herself the one person in operatic London. She and her husband used to say, " Catalani, three or four puppets, and there you have all that is wanted." In 1815 the French King invited her over to Paris to manage the Théatre Italien; she managed it badly, cutting everything down except her own fees and personal opportunities. From 1817 to 1827 she lived a roving life, singing in Germany, Austria, Russia, and England, and gradually fading.

But her hold on the public did not fail. When on July 21st, 1821, after a six years' absence, she reappeared in England, her concert was " liberally patronized by the Dukes of Clarence and Cambridge, the Princess Augusta, and the Duchesses of Gloucester and Cambridge, and also by an immense number of the nobility." The room " glittered with stars and orders, notwithstanding the music for the Coronation of George IV was being rehearsed at Carlton House, and Mr. and Mrs. Coutts had a grand concert and ball at their residence on the same evening."

You and I could not have got into Catalani's concert in the Argyle Rooms, and so should not

From the Ceci collection

MADAME CATALANI

have heard her sing the new grand air by the Marquis Sampieri, of which the title was *Della superba Roma ;* or Rode's famous air with variations; or Pucetta's recitative and air, *Mio bene ;* or the single verse of *God Save the King ;* or Mozart's *Non più andrai* (a piece familiar to us by many bass singers, into which the soprano, besides carrying it up a few octaves, introduced alterations and embellishments in the approved manner). We should have missed all this wonderful music, and we should not have been able to note that " the singer sang with greater effort, the agitation of the muscles of her face, and the motion of the lower jaw, particularly in her shake, which had always been painful to observe, being evidently much increased."

Some Beethoven sonatas had recently come into the country, and we should probably have contented ourselves with these.

In 1828 Angelica Catalani retired. She bought a place near Florence, where she lived for awhile. Then she removed to Paris, there to die, 1849, of cholera. I imagine she quickly faded out of remembrance, when once retired; because the obituary notices written in 1843, on the occasion of an incorrect report of her death, were for the most part curiously brief and conventional.

II

Giudetta Pasta was a woman very much

MAKERS OF MUSIC

unlike Catalani : indeed, her character, in every
way—personal and artistic—fills one with admiration.

She was so fine and true an actress that people
called her the Mrs. Siddons of the operatic stage,
and the greatest actors used to say with surprise
that they could for once learn something further
of their art from a singer. Such a record is so
rare as to be almost unique.* Then as a singer
she had many disadvantages all through her life,
while the beginning of her public work seems
to have been quite a failure. The initial failure
she overcame by continued hard work; so that
where in 1816 she and her husband together
could only command £400 for a season, six or
seven years later she alone could command
£14,000. The defects of her singing she overcame by the force of her acting, so that though
she might sing flat the audience scarcely noticed
the harshness.

Born at Como in 1798, of a Jewish family of
the name of Negri, Giudetta started early to sing
in the minor Italian theatres, gradually making
her way to Paris and London. Her voice
was a heavy mezzo soprano, very untractable,
and not particularly pleasant. She was about
twenty when she realized that some very hard
work was wanted before success could be won;
and so she went back to Italy to study. Within
a few years her voice became a soprano, and it

* See page 232

334

became a more manageable thing; though she was always better in the *mezzo voce* than the full voice.

Her manner was extraordinarily noble; eyes, mouth, and forehead were formed in the high classic mould of drama, and her acting was less acting than the natural living of the part. She moved serious people as profoundly as the ordinary excitable member of the operatic audience: thus Barry Cornwall wrote to her some of the finest poetry ever addressed to a musician, and it was generally said that she dignified the art of opera.

I will copy a few lines from Barry Cornwall's poem :

I see thee at all hours, beneath all skies,
   In every shape thou tak'st, or passionate path ;
Now thou art like some wingèd thing that cries
    Over a city flaming fast to death.
Now in thy voice the mad Medea dies,
   Now Desdemona yields her gentle breath ;
All things thou art by turns, from wrath to love,
   From the queen-eagle to the vestal dove.

Having a fine dramatic intelligence, Pasta had the fine understanding of the " word," and so her articulation was perfect. If a singer sings so that you cannot pick out the sentences, it is generally because the singer has rather an obscured intellectuality; no one articulates well but one who has the poetic intelligence, and they say that Pasta's *recitativo parlante* was clearer even than a good actor's speaking of the lines.

She bought a villa on the Lake of Como in 1829, and when not engaged in singing gave up her time to a beautiful garden, which was her joy and pride.

Moscheles gives us a picture of Pasta in retirement, in the year 1853, when she was fifty-five. " This famous cantatrice lives in a small house adjoining her own villa, on the lake of Como. Close to the door we stumbled on some prosaic matters—dirty saucepans, kitchen utensils, and the like, not to mention the leavings of an early dinner. Amid this débris sat three unkempt girls, not one of them in love with soap and water. At my bidding one of them took in our cards, and the great lady soon appeared. We did not see her at her best, for having just risen from her siesta in which we had disturbed her, she was only half awake. We found her very friendly, and evidently gratified with our visit. Her mouth and teeth are still lovely, the great eyes full of fire, her black hair was in a dishevelled state, and her dress an extremely original medley of oddities. She never ceased talking of old times, and told us she had given up living in the villa, because both her mother and her husband had died there. She afterwards wrote something for our albums, and gave us some beautiful flowers."

Another writer shows us Pasta once more. He

MALIBRAN

says: " On passing by the steamboat plying between Colico and Como, I saw her for the last time, late one evening in August, 1861, driving a string of twelve or more turkeys with a long stick towards their roosting-place." The year of her death was 1865.

III

The Garcias were a famous family, of whom the most famous member was Malibran: her name is still mentioned with a curiously individual effect, although she died at the age of twenty-eight.

The first Garcia was Manuel del Popolo Vicente, born 1775, died 1832. He was a good tenor singer, with a voice of unusual size and of great range, and an actor of fine dramatic intelligence. Starting from Seville, his birth-place, and supported by an iron will, Garcia gradually made himself famous in France, Italy and England (less so in England than elsewhere), as an operatic singer, operatic manager, and operatic composer. He was very proud of his position, and as proud of his teaching as of any-thing else. He was the sternest of stern masters, whoever might be his pupils; but to his children he was more than stern, being cruel, and affording them no recreation.

His son Manuel was born in Madrid in 1805, to die in London in 1906, seventy years later than his younger sister Malibran. He invented the laryngoscope, and was a great teacher for three-quarters of a century. His wife, Eugenia, did well in opera about the year 1843. Among his pupils was Jenny Lind.

Maria Felicità, the great Malibran, was born in 1808. Her debut took place in 1825, but without attracting much notice. Four years later she made an astonishing leap into fame, partly by reason of her beautiful contralto voice, but mainly by the emotional energy she put into her work. Her name of Malibran comes of her marriage (in New York, in 1827, during her father's tour in America) with a French merchant. This marriage was dissolved in France, after which Maria married De Bériot, the violinist.

So great was the energy with which she sang and acted, that often at the close of a performance she collapsed and lay insensible. No companion actor satisfied her who was not impassioned.— *" Good heavens, sir, don't you know you are my lover ? You must make love to me with some show of passion in the first act, and in the second you must pull me about the stage as if you would tear me into little bits."* " But, madame, I shall hurt you." *" And what if you do ? Never you mind. That is my affair, and if you don't do it, by heaven I'll kill you."* And she stamped her foot, until the actor thought she would surely do so.

In 1836 Malibran rode a dangerous horse, meeting with an accident. Soon after she sang

THE GARCIAS

at the Manchester Festival : the strain of singing, combined with the after-effects of the accident— and particularly the special effort to surpass another singer at the festival—caused a breakdown. The doctors treated her wrongly, bleeding a person who wanted all the blood nature could provide, and she died almost immediately. M. de Bériot did not wait for the funeral to take place at Manchester: by French law, her first husband might have claimed that part of her property which was in France, and De Bériot was anxious to get his hand on this before the news of the woman's death reached Paris.

Pauline Garcia was born in 1821, to live on into the year 1910. She was a mezzo-soprano, and a great actress. In 1859, when she was in the prime of her powers, Gluck's *Orfée* was revived in Paris; and it received a hundred and fifty consecutive performances. Her husband was the director of the Paris opera, but on their marriage (in 1840) he gave up that work and managed his wife's tours. She is always referred to as Madame Viardot-Garcia. There were four clever musicians among the children of this marriage, though none has become generally famous.

IV

History is curiously self-willed, and sometimes plays pranks, omitting to record the work of a praiseworthy musician, and balancing the matter by incorporating an account of a musician who never did any notable work at all.

This perversity is illustrated by the case of Emma Howson, known as Madame Albertazzi, from her marriage (at the age of sixteen) to a lawyer of Piacenza. She was born in 1814, and began to sing in public at the age of fifteen ; that is, in 1829. Although she studied under good masters, her voice remained ill-trained ; and it was of a thin quality. She was pretty, unassuming, and (as contemporary writers are careful to say) ladylike ; which pleased the audience ; but on the stage she was most irritatingly tame, moving about in a weary, resigned, and indeed indifferent manner, as if she had no intellectual, let alone any dramatic, interest in the opera or in her part. She was almost an automaton, the opposite of Malibran. And the decorations she applied to her melodies were disjoined and apparently casual.

The following represents the best kind of criticism she received :

On Monday evening (July 17th) an English version of Rossini's opera, *La Gazza Ladra*, was produced at the Princess's Theatre, the character of Annette being played by Madame Albertazzi. Of the various Italian operas which have, in an English form, been brought forward at this theatre, the present adaptation

330

ALBERTAZZI

is the least praiseworthy. Madame Albertazzi's
singing was marked throughout by considerable taste and sweetness, but even her admirers
must have felt some regret that she did not
act with more expression and animation. Her
performance was evidently the result of study,
but it appeared that she had studied the music
alone, not directing her energies toward a
perfect embodiment of the character, which
presents many opportunities for effective display, but which, on this occasion, were not
exercised to advantage. The finale was most
charmingly sung by this lady, and the audience
were so loud in their applause that it was
almost impossible to avoid an encore.—
Pictorial Times, July 22nd, 1843.

Yet this singer is most regularly referred to
in histories and dictionaries ; and she was quite
successful in opera in Italy, Spain, France, and
her native country—successful, that is, in getting
engagements, and profitable ones at that.

Here is one of the " topical paragraphs "
which in those days used to attend the path of
the singer well-known to the public :

Madame Albertazzi is daily expected in
London. Such is the competition among the
principal London managers for the possession
of talent of a superior kind that one enter-
prising *entrepreneur* has stationed persons at

331

the Custom-house, waiting the arrival of the packets, and armed with authority to treat at once with the accomplished vocalist.—*Ib.*, March 25th, 1843.

Later in the year 1843 her voice began to fail, and the critics note with regret her " growing languor and repugnance to exertion, which she more and more manifests every day," seeing therein signs of serious illness. The fact was, that consumption had marked her for its own, and she was doomed to die in 1847, when only thirty-three years old.

It is not, however, any sentimental regard for this sad fate which has kept her name forward in musical history, but simply the freakish will of the spirit of record.

XXVIII. CLARA NOVELLO

Sixteen years ago, in the early part of 1908, died a woman singer on whose famous " high B flat " Charles Lamb, the most musical of all unmusical people, made jokes, and whose singing amazed the German world around Mendelssohn in the year Queen Victoria came to the throne.

This was Clara Anastasia Novello, who was born in 1818, and was ninety when—after nearly fifty years of retirement—she died.

I

The Novellos were an interesting family. Vincent, the father, was a well-known and useful London musician, a man of general interests in music and of wide culture, and a publisher whose work led to the famous publishing house of Novello & Co.

His wife was Mary Sabilla Hehl. There were eleven children, Clara being the fourth. Mary, one of the daughters, married Charles Cowden Clarke, and we know of her in literature under the name of Mrs. Cowden Clarke. One of the sons, Alfred, was a good public singer, but his chief work was in the construction of his father's publishing business. Another sister married J. T. Serle, a literary man connected with the drama ; she likewise sang in public. Yet another sister, by name Sabilla, was a good public singer ; and a brother named Edward Petre was a clever painter, but died when only twenty-two.

333

MAKERS OF MUSIC

In a smaller measure, the home of Vincent Novello was like the home of Dr. Burney in the preceding generation ; that is, it was a place to which literary men and artists used to go, as well as musicians : he numbered among his friends Lamb and Lamb's sister, Shelley, Keats, Leigh Hunt, Hazlitt, Edward Holmes (who wrote the first English life of Mozart), Cowden Clarke naturally, Copley Fielding, and many others we meet with in the smaller chronicles of the time.

Clara is the most famous of the Novello family, as she was the most gifted.

There was plenty of high spirits, fun, and wit in the social life of this family, as always where Charles Lamb entered.

Lamb refers frequently to these friends of his, and pokes fun at their concentrated interest in music. The *Elia* essay, "A Chapter on Ears," mentions them, also many of his letters. The letter to William Ayrton, dated only *Thursday*, but belonging to 1830, contains the bright little poem which begins :

> Some cry up Haydn, some Mozart,
> Just as the whim bites. For my part,
> I do not care a farthing candle
> For either of them, nor for Handel.

Lamb wrote the poem (so he says, at least) in response to Novello's wish that he should give him his real opinion of Eminent Composers.

CLARA NOVELLO

The following letter is a delightful joke ; it teases Vincent on his antiquarian work :

[*About May* 20*th*, 1830]

DEAR N.,—Pray write immediately, to say " The book has come safe." I am curious not so much for the autographs as for that bit of the hair-brush. I enclose a cinder, which belonged to *Shield* when he was poor, and lit his own fires. Any memorial of a great musical genius, I know, is acceptable ; and Shield has his merits, though Clementi, in my opinion, is far above him in the *sostenuto*.

Mr. Westwood desires his compliments, and begs to present you with a nail that came out of Jomelli's coffin, who is buried at Naples.

II

Clara was thus born into a home where music was going on constantly, and she picked it up just as we ordinary folk, ordinarily circumstanced, pick up language. More than this, she picked it up to perfection, not haltingly in the way we learn to speak ; and when only three years old she surprised her father by suddenly singing, from beginning to end, a popular aria she had heard played in the street ; it was the *Di tanti palpiti*.

Vincent Novello looked carefully after the child, and when she went to school (in York) she was already, at the age of nine, a trained musician.

Schooling in York only lasted a year or two, because Vincent heard there was a vacancy for a pupil in a singing school for classical and religious music which was established in Paris. Time was short, but the child was taken quickly over to Paris, and after only three days of preparation, competed successfully for the admission.

There were nineteen candidates. Clara was the youngest. But she took first place easily, amusing the judges by her calm, businesslike manner as much as she surprised them by her singing : this was in 1829, when she was eleven ; but anyone who without seeing her heard her sing thought it must be a girl of sixteen or eighteen.

Unfortunately for this course of study, the Revolution of 1830 broke out the next year ; and all children like Clara Novello had to be brought away. This child was impressionable : things of beauty and character stamped themselves permanently on her mind, and things of horror, such as the fighting in the streets of Paris, made her seriously ill. It was many months before she recovered from the effects of sights seen during the Revolution.

Back in London, she studied further under Moscheles the pianist and Costa the conductor ; and then, in 1832, the father took her to various

336

CLARA NOVELLO

towns in the country—Windsor, Oxford, Liverpool, Dublin, etc.—there to sing at concerts.

Clara's success was complete. Some of the better-known English singers of the time performed in the concerts, yet the fourteen-year-old girl held her own with them, taking parts in duets and glees as well as singing solos.

Her chief pieces were Handel's " Hush, ye pretty warbling Choir," and two pieces by her father, " O'er hill and dale " and " The Infant's Prayer." The famous B flat of her voice was now developed ; it rang clear and full like a bell, and with a miraculous steadiness. The people liked her calm and collected manner, and her youthful appearance touched them ; but they rather ridiculed the peculiar way she did her hair and the somewhat fantastic manner of her dress for the platform.

The mediæval buildings of Oxford deeply moved her ; she and her father stayed there some days, so that she could thoroughly absorb the beauty of architecture, and for many years Clara Novello used to speak of that experience.

We do not all learn to respond to the art of architecture ; but musicians ought to cultivate understanding of it equally with understanding of poetry : poetry quickens our intellectual faculties, thereby helping us to grasp the finer details of music ; and architecture, by quickening our sense of form, helps us to apprehend its larger details. I have no doubt that those few days in Oxford did more for Clara Novello than all the public singing of the " tournée," as such a provincial engagement was then called.

III

Great honours came to the girl at once. At the Christmas of this year (1832) Beethoven's D major Mass had its first performance in London, and she was engaged to sing among the soloists. Then came engagements to appear at all the important London meetings—the Ancient Concerts, the Vocal Concerts, and the Philharmonic Society's Concerts. The year of 1833 was her first great year. It was the year in which Mara died at Reval, and Todi in Lisbon, and when the great Italian singers of the day were in their supreme power—singers with whom she was to stand equal before long.

This success continued in England for several years. Provincial festivals, as those of Worcester and Hull, called her no less than London concerts ; and the strain of travelling was great, though Clara, like all other popular performers, was very strong.

Lamb, now in the last year of his life, was moved by her singing, and wrote to her the poem which begins,

> The Gods have made me most unmusical,
> With feelings that respond not to the call
> Of stringèd harp, or voice,

CLARA NOVELLO

and which ends,

> Yet do I admire,
> O tuneful daughter of a tuneful sire !
> Thy painful labours in a science which
> To your deserts I pray may make you rich
> As much as you are loved, and add a grace
> To the most musical Novello race.
> Women lead men by the nose, some cynics say ;
> You draw them by the ear—a delicater way !

He also made one of his jocular criticisms on her work : there was a Royal Musical Festival held in Westminster Abbey at the end of June, 1834, at which Clara sang ; and Lamb wrote thus to Cowden Clarke :

> We heard the music in the Abbey, at Winchmore Hill, and the notes were incomparably softened by the distance. Novello's chromatics [he played the organ] were distinctly audible. Clara was faulty in B flat. Otherwise she sang like an angel.

IV

Our artist, now nineteen years old, was ambitious to be great in opera as in oratorio and concert-singing. She also craved the pleasure of fame in Italy ; and so plans were made for her to go abroad.

Alfred, and probably his father, wanted her to go straight to Italy, there to study opera-singing for a while, after which triumphs were to be won in the theatres of Italy, France, and England. But Mendelssohn, who was often with the Novellos when visiting England, persuaded them that it would be good for Clara to sing in Germany first.

And so Clara went to Germany, to experience a most brilliant success. She was away till 1843 —nearly six years.

I can here tell the story of her Continental life better by direct quotations than by ordinary narrative, because what was written at the time is first-hand material, with the clear personality of the writers and the warm tone of a record of immediate happening. Clara first sang in Germany at the Gewandhaus concert on November 2nd, 1837 ; this was at Leipzig, where Mendelssohn was director of music.

Schumann wrote as follows of her singing at the Gewandhaus concerts :

Miss Clara Novello was the most interesting of these [artists who took part in the orchestral concerts]. She came to us from her friendly London circle, heralded as an artist of the first rank, which weighed with us in Leipzig. I have for years heard nothing to please me more than this voice, predominating over all the other tones, yet breathing a tender euphony, every tone sharply defined like the tones of a keyed instrument, aided by the noble performance, the simplicity, yet art, which seemed to desire the elevation of the composer and his work only. . . . From such a performer the composer himself may learn : when we hear it, we feel again respect for the executive artist, who so often gives us caricatures, because he leaves school too soon. Art such as this snaps asunder at once the stilts on which stalks ordinary virtuosity, thinking to look over our shoulders. Miss Clara Novello is not a Malibran, nor yet a Sontag, but she has her own high original individuality, of which no one can deprive her.

On the 19th of the month Mendelssohn wrote a long letter to Alfred about his sister's success : this was printed in *The Musical Times* for April, 1908, and it contained the following passages (written in English):

. . . it comes now out how well I know my countrymen, how well they appreciate what is really good and beautiful, and what a service to all the lovers of music has been done by your sister's coming over to this country. I do not know whether she thinks the same of my opinion now, I am sometimes afraid she must find the place so very small and dull, and miss her splendid philharmonic band and all those marchionesses and duchesses and lady patronesses who look so beautifully aristocratically in your Concert-rooms, and of whom we have a great want. But if being really heartily liked and loved by a public, and being looked on as a most distinguished and eminent talent must also convey a feeling of pleasure to those that are the object of it— I am sure that your sister cannot repent her resolution of accepting the invitation to this place, and must be glad to think of the delight she gave and the many friends she made in so short a time and in a foreign country. Indeed I never heard such an unanimous expression of delight, as after her first Recitative, and it was a pleasure to see people at once agreeing and the difference of opinion (which must always prevail) consisting in the more or less praise to be bestowed on her. It was capital that not one hand's applause received her when she first appeared to sing " non più di fiore," because the triumph after the Recitative was the greater ; *the room rung of applause, and after it there was such a noise of conversations, people expressing their delight to each other, that not a note of the whole ritornelle could be heard ; then silence was again restored,* and after the air, which she really sang better and with more expression than I ever heard from her, my good Leipzig public became like mad, and made a most tremendous noise. Since that moment she was the declared favourite of them, they are equally delighted with her clear and youthful voice and with the purity and good taste with which she sings everything. The Polacca of the Puritani was encored, which is a rare thing in our Concerts here, and I am quite sure the longer she stays and the more she is heard the more she will become a favourite ; because she possesses just those two qualities of which the public is particularly fond here, purity of intonation and a thoroughbred musical feeling. . . . And now the paper is over and consequently the letter also. Excuse its style, which is probably very German. . . .

v

The " ritornelle " mentioned in that part of the quotation which I have put in italics, is the instrumental passage connecting a recitative with its aria. You will observe that Mendelssohn says the audience applauded, talked, and buzzed through it, so that not a note of the instrumental passage was heard. They did this, because in those days the singer, not the song, was what counted : the instrumental introductions and interludes, like the *tutti* passages in a concerto, were merely recreative passages where the performer of the solo part recovered. Now when you read in your history books that composers (Haydn, Mozart, etc.) are inclined to the habit of using only conventional music in the linking-

343

up parts of sonatas, filling the space between one
melody or subject and another with meaningless
runs and arpeggios—and when your historian
tells you that these composers ought to be
ashamed of such laziness, you may be satisfied
that he has not arrived at the philosophy of the
matter : a hundred or more years ago people
used to applaud in the middle of a piece ; a nice
modulation, a particularly sweet melody, or a
graceful cadence, and at once they clapped their
hands, and spoke audibly of their pleasure, the
while the music continued : therefore the composers did not trouble to write good music in the
links and connections, because nobody wanted
good music there, and if good music were
provided it would not be heard. The symphonies
of Haydn and Mozart are supplied with good
solid pauses of silence, in order to give people a
clear opportunity to applaud in the middle of a
movement and to make convenient the sectional
encore which was likely to be asked for. The
length of a *tutti* in a concerto was determined
by the composer on the assumption, first that the
performer would want so long to rest, and
secondly on the assumption that the audience
would want so long to applaud at the end of the
solo passage preceding the *tutti*.* We do not
now applaud in this manner, and of late we
prefer to listen to a symphony with no applause
even between the movements ; but if you go to

* See *Masters of Music,* page 244.

a vocal concert in a pothouse, or to an entertainment in a village schoolroom, you will find that the applause of Mendelssohn's generation still prevails, and that the audience clap their hands on the last note of each verse, sustaining the sound steadily while the pianist gets through the interlude, and stopping it sharp as the edge of a knife the moment the singer makes the first note of the next verse.

Therefore it was a sign of Clara Novello's supreme success that this ritornello was not audible between her first recitative and its aria ; and the audience were not rude to composer and band.

We do not, it appears, breed singers of this type to-day, except accidentally, because our present interest (since Wagner) is more in the music. The general tastes of the time when great singers were active encouraged them to pull the music about in order to make better display-material of it, and to ignore the poesy of the art : Clara Novello, adopting custom, sometimes allowed herself to make changes in the written melody ; but as a rule she was a true artist.

VI

After the brilliant start at Leipzig, the rest of Germany was easy travelling. Berlin, Weimar (where the Grand Duchess was a pupil of Hummel), Vienna, and other capitals, made as

345

much of her as Mendelssohn's place. In Berlin
they granted her the diploma of the chief musical
society, Clara being the first of all women to be so
honoured (she was already an elected associate
of the London Philharmonic Society); and the
Crown Prince on every possible occasion asked
her to sing " I know that my Redeemer liveth."

The Empress of Russia being sister to the
Crown Prince, Miss Novello was sent to Petersburg with the warmest letters of recommendation,
which served finally to clear the path to the
Russian Court already opened by her German
successes—

. . . And condescendingly flattering indeed
was the greeting thus ensured at the court of
St. Petersburg. Her Imperial Majesty seemed
to take peculiar pleasure in marking the high
esteem she entertained towards the young
artiste, not only as regarded her talent, but
also on account of her private character,
placing her by her own side on the ottoman,
and after making her explain and illustrate the
different styles of English and Scotch national
music, said, " Oh, now sing me something
German." Upon Clara Novello's complying
by singing the lively air, " Mein chastz ist
ein Reiter," the Empress smiled delightedly,
exclaiming, " Ah, that's what I used to sing
myself, when I was a mädchen in Berlin ! "
In short, it was with reluctance that the singer

declined the brilliant offers which were made her to remain in Russia, with a noble pension for life, as prima donna, being now anxious to prosecute her original intention of visiting Italy.

Thus wrote a member of the staff of *The Dramatic and Musical Review* for April 8th, 1843, who waited on the singer when, in that year, she came back to London, to gather from her an account of her experiences abroad.

To Italy Miss Novello went, in the year 1839. First she studied for the operatic stage in Milan, having help from Rossini and the great singer Pasta among others. Then she made her debut, in *Semiramide*, at Padua, to leap at once into a further fame.

After Padua came Bologna, Genoa, Modena, Milan, Rome and Fermo, in which last-named place Clara met her future husband, Count Gigluicci. The Genoese engaged her for the year following, and out of this engagement developed a pretty little contest between two cities.

VII

Before describing this contest, however, which I shall do by a further quotation from *The Dramatic and Musical Review* article (in which quotation will come a picture of Miss Novello's

Italian successes) I should say that she ran back
to Germany in the end of 1839, for a slightly
—what shall I call it ? Spiteful ?—purpose.
Mrs. Alfred Shaw, a very fine singer, had been
appearing in Leipzig, and Mendelssohn had
said that she and Clara were the two finest heard
in the place for a long while. Such harnessed
praise was hardly good enough for the younger
of the two ; and so she planned to sing in the
town immediately after Mrs. Shaw had made
one of her appearances. This, if not spiteful,
was not generous, though excusable enough in
politics, business, singing, acting, and the like.

Mendelssohn mentions the matter in a letter
to his sister, dated October 11th, 1839 :

> We have new pianists, alas ! for all the
> concerts up to Christmas, and among them
> are some queer specimens. Next week we have
> a competition of singers which is really quite
> alarming. Madame Löwe from Berlin, and
> Mme. Botgorschek from Dresden, Mme.
> Shaw from London, and Miss Novello from
> Milan, all meet here and make the Gewandhaus
> their battle-field. Novello is coming, I believe,
> on purpose to play a trick on Shaw (a " Shawber-
> nack," if I may take a leaf out of Hensel's
> book). She has written a lot of letters from
> Italy, leaving me to pay the postage, announces
> a concert two days after Mme. Shaw's first,
> and then goes to Prussia.

CLARA NOVELLO

Thus we are shown that Clara was fully "capable." She saved money on her correspondence, by leaving postage to be paid by the receiver (as was then an alternative custom), and she shattered the just-acquired credit of her rivals by cool and businesslike methods.

VIII

Now for the lengthy extract from *The Dramatic and Musical Review* for 1843, in which we can hear the voice of Clara as she talks with her interviewer :

". . . The autumn season at Bologna was her next engagement. . . . Twenty-seven successive performances [of *Lucrezia Borgia*] left the Bolognese still unsatiated ; she was unanimously created a member of the Philharmonic Society, one of the most ancient in Italy. Rossini, for the first time for many years, frequently attended the opera. The impresario at Genoa immediately secured her for the ensuing Carnival there, to repeat this same opera, and out of the thirty-seven nights which form the season, *Lucrezia* was performed thirty. Before Miss Novello left Genoa, she was compelled to promise that she would return the following year. Rossini was now about to give the grand performance of his *Stabat Mater*, for the first time in Italy. The

choice of all the *prime donne* in Italy being
given to the great composer on this memorable
occasion, he distinguished Miss Novello by
immediately naming her.   When Rossini
first heard her rehearse the celebrated solo
' Inflammatus,' and hold out the concluding
E *in alt*, with that ease and volume of tone
which are so peculiarly her own, he rushed to
embrace her, exclaiming, ' Ora son contento ! '*
Modena next claimed Miss Novello . . . on
her benefit, besides munificent presents, the
Grand Duke ordered a *bouquet monstre* to be
culled from his own private garden, an un-
precedented honour from this potentate.

" We have before mentioned that Clara
Novello had been re-engaged at Genoa ; but
the Roman public having declared that they
would listen to no other singer but ' the
Novello,' the manager [at Rome] resolved to
try every method for securing the favourite
cantatrice.   In vain did he protest she was
engaged elsewhere ; the answer was, ' Then
you may shut your theatre, for even if an
angiolo were to sing for us, we would hear
nobody but *la Novello !* ' In this extremity,
stratagem was resorted to ; the impresario
pretended a previous engagement, and immediately commenced a lawsuit, and Clara

---

*" Now I am satisfied." It really does one good to read of
these things—of such perfect successes, such genuine approvals,
and such universal life and warmth.

CLARA NOVELLO

Novello being then in the Roman states, was
detained there until the cause was decided.
The court was held at Rome, some of the
judges being relations of the manager, and
all of them anxious to hear the artiste who
was contested by two such cities; the decision
may hence easily be guessed. Genoa protested
violently against this foppery, as they considered it, and a dispute arose which might
have ended somewhat tragically, had not the
British authorities interposed in favour of
their countrywoman, and settled that she
should be equally divided between the two
theatres. This was agreed to by all parties,
and Clara Novello proceeded to Rome, where
she was to sing during the first half of the
Carnival season. Any unjust or tyrannical
conduct was now amply compensated by the
furore her appearance created. Her own
compatriots, proud of their ' Syren of Albion,'
as she was commonly termed, forgot their
national *froideur*, and rivalled the enthusiastic
Italians in their demonstrations of admiration.
On her benefit [the ' benefit ' for the favourite
singer was generally the climax of an engage-
ment] the furore was almost appalling ; after
her singing the *Casta Diva* from *Norma*, she
was called on no fewer than twenty-nine times.
[Who was it that retained presence of mind
to keep count of these recalls ? I imagine
Clara herself, who was always calm and

collected.] On her entering a box to hear
Moriani in his dying scene, the whole audience
rose, stood on the benches to obtain a view of
their idol, and continued applauding and
cheering. On her return home, the horses
were taken from her carriage, and she was
carried home in triumph, accompanied by all
the first nobles in Rome, bearing torches.
The marble hall, entrance, and staircase,
were lined with admirers, who greeted her
with loud *evvivas !* while a fine military band
played all her most celebrated airs. So dense
was the crowd, and so loud the shouts, that
many peaceful inhabitants were wakened out
of their sleep, fearing some revolution, until
the repeated shouts of *Viva la Novello,* etc.,
acquainted them with the joyous nature of the
tumult. She was repeatedly compelled to
shew herself in the balcony, to receive fresh
bursts of applause, while ladies in full dress
waved handkerchiefs and threw flowers from
their carriage windows. On the following
morning, she received a solemn deputation,
bringing her a diploma, naming her a member
of the Philharmonic Society of St. Cecilia—
which society numbers monarchs among its
members. On her departure, the way through
which she passed was lined with carriages,
from which ladies waved their handkerchiefs,
while shouts of ' Return to us, Novello ! '
rent the air. Sonnets, and every kind of

CLARA NOVELLO

elegant verse, were employed to deplore her departure and sing her praises. From Rome she travelled day and night to Genoa, where her old friends received her with open arms. A new opera was written expressly for the Pet of the Romans, as she was now styled. . . . Warmly did the Genoese wish that their favourite might be induced to prolong her visit . . . but an engagement in her own native land compelled her to refuse their generous offers. Amid kind regrets, and repeated injunctions to ' Return to Genoa, la Superba ! ' she set sail for England."

This eighty-year old passage conveys to us the very soul of the times. We see cities fighting for the services of a singer who pleases, and resorting to neat little legal dishonesties to get their end. We see pleasure developed to excitement, and thence to frenzy, with military bands, bouquets, and packed crowds. And through it all moves Clara Novello, or whoever else is the favoured one, with " her own strong mind and extensive acquirements," almost without doubt calculating how soon such success will enable her to retire. For these people did not live for a great, impersonal art.

MAKERS OF MUSIC

IX

Clara Novello came to London, where she made her debut in an opera by Giovanni Pacini (1796-1867). This opera, *Saffo*, was the best of the composer's ninety works for the stage. It had been given in Naples three years earlier, and was now done into English for Clara's benefit by her brother-in-law, J. T. Serle, and mounted at Drury Lane by Macready.

There was a good deal of excitement over the production. Mrs. Shaw had an important part, and she and Miss Novello had a duet, " Ah ! fate unhappy ! " Among the second tenors was a singer of whom a critic, with the eternal brilliance of the minor members of the craft, said that " Mr. J. Reeves' rich tenor was heard to great advantage, though in a small part." This singer afterwards altered his name from *J. Reeves* to *Sims Reeves*.

The waves in the last scene were badly managed, giving the impression that several different winds must be blowing simultaneously. Apart from this elemental error, *Sappho* was a great success, and Miss Novello " elicited loud and well-merited applause."

During this year, Miss Novello sang in a stage performance of Handel's *Acis and Galatea*, then in the Sacred Harmonic Society's performance of the *Messiah*, and lastly at the Birmingham Festival.

CLARA NOVELLO

As pendant to the second of these engagements, I read the following in *The Dramatic and Musical Review* :

> We have received several indignant remonstrances against the " contemptuous demeanour " of this favourite vocalist, at the Sacred Harmonic Concert, on Friday evening, at Exeter Hall. Although it is a nice point to criticize the demeanour of public singers, we fear that there were some grounds for the displeasure of the audience in the manner in which they were treated by Miss Novello. We wish no vocalist to be unduly imposed on by the public, who are too often exacting and inconsiderate in the extent of their demands, but we do entreat Miss Novello not to stand in the way of her own fame ; and to pause before she offends a public as yet so prepossessed in her favour.

This sounds rather dreadful. What contempt had she revealed by her demeanour ? And why this rather guarded criticism, reproach, and recommendation ? But when I read the passage a second time, I saw that this spoiled darling of Italy, Germany, and the Russian Court had truly been most unpardonably insulting. She had robbed the audience of encores.

No greater wrong could have been done them, because her denial meant that those present were having to pay, say, sixpence a head for each song, as against threepence by means of repetitions.*

At the end of the year Miss Novello married Count Gigliucci and, leaving music, went to live in Italy. She was then twenty-five. The political troubles of 1848 drove her back, because her husband's property was confiscated by the Austrian Government. Until 1860 she sang in Italy, Lisbon, and England—chiefly in the great Handel Celebrations at the new Crystal Palace, where her voice was of wonderful power, able to fill the entire place ; and then she retired a second time, to live peacefully for nearly fifty years in Rome and Fermo.

She made her farewell appearance at the age of forty-two, and died at the age of ninety.

* " There was a strange scene the other evening, when the ' Messiah' was given. Those excellent artistes, Clara Novello and Mrs. Shaw, stirred the audience to great enthusiasm ; it literally rained encores. Mrs. Shaw seemed willing to comply with the wishes of the audience, Miss Novello the reverse ; she withstood all the shouts, clapping of hands, and other noisy demonstrations, and Phillips' song, ' Why do the heathen rage ? ' seemed well suited to the occasion, and was only half listened to by an audience shouting ' Miss Novello ! ', ' encore ! '. It was no good, she declined to repeat her song, and left the orchestra. At last the music was allowed to proceed without interruption, and when it came to the heavenly air, ' I know that my Redeemer liveth,' Miss Novello stepped forward again, this time accompanied by a member of the committee, who was about to speak, but someone shouted out ' bad temper,' and the Witches' Sabbath began afresh, so that the poor lady sang the greater part of her sublime song amidst the alternate hisses, applause, and screams of the audience. At last, however, her fine singing prevailed, and the turmoil was at an end." This account, which makes vividly clear the character of our national " froideur " was written by Mrs. Moscheles.

XXIX. CONCLUSION

I

A brilliant body of singers were at work around the year 1843, every member worthy of study. But space here allows no more than a concluding mention of their names. The chief of these were Madame Caradori-Allan (1800-1865), who sang in the first performance of *Elijah* ; Wilhelmine Schröder-Devrient (1804-1860), a remarkable dramatic singer who fills many pages of the history of her times, and was in contact with Beethoven, Weber, Mendelssohn, and Wagner, her life's work embracing *Fidelio* and *Tannhäuser* ; Henriette Sontag (1804-1854), one of the first German singers who made their way into the Italian stronghold ; Julie Dorus Gras, the Frenchwoman (1807-1896), Fanny Persiani (1812-1867), to whose name—as to the name of many another singer—is attached the story of a row in the theatre.

This was the period of that wonderful quartet —Giulia Grisi (1811-1869), Antonio Tamburini (1800-1876), Giuseppe Mario (1810-1883), and Luigi Lablache (1794-1858)—who sang together in opera, and who, it is pretty certain, have never been matched, and scarcely ever can be matched, since we no longer train singers in their manner.

Innumerable other names remain remembered —Bassano, Miss Birch, Burdini, Conti (a failure), Fornasari (who electrified London, driving the

357

critics into a lyric rapture), Harrison (a favourite tenor), Moltini, Miss Poole, Miss Rainforth, Weiss (the composer of *The Village Blacksmith*), Ronza di Begnis (a woman of dazzling beauty), John Templeton, Joseph Staudigl, Rubini (who was in Russia in 1843, at the same time as Liszt was touring there, with whom he shared paragraphs in all the papers, showing that he was equally famous), Benedetta Pisaroni, Mary Ann Paton (just now retired for a time to a convent in York), Mrs. Salmon (already broken down and destitute, however, her curse being an incurable drunkenness : she used to come drunk on the platform, and be laughed off by the audience) ; Miss Stephens (who, when she was forty-four, married an earl, aged about eighty-five, and after his death lived for forty or fifty years on the profits) ; Duprez (he shared with Rubini the honour of much newspaper paragraphing) ; Mrs. Alfred Shaw—named above . . . and so many others, that one could fill a dozen pages with their names and chronologies all once passionate and eager musicians, who have managed to strike a vibration in history, and who can teach us a lesson or afford us a few minutes of entertaining reading, but are otherwise finished.

Out in the brilliancy of the footlights—filling the attention of perhaps a crowded audience, and making many a breath and pulse swell and rise—

CONCLUSION

O so much passion and imparted life !—over
and over again, the season through—walking,
gesticulating, singing, reciting his or her part—
But then sooner or later inevitably wending to
the flies or exit door—vanishing to sight and ear
—and never materializing on this earth's stage
again !

II

I had intended in this section of my book
presenting the young reader with a full survey
of all the great line of singers, so that when he
or she met a name, when reading history, bio-
graphy, or letters of musicians, that name could
be made real by a reference to one of my pages.

But the singers were too many, and several
seduced me into telling their story at some length ;
and so my space has gone, while I am yet in the
other half of the nineteenth century.

En ough, however, will have been done if
these pages help you to realize the living character
of all great performers, and if from them you can
learn to vitalize the rather meagre records given
in the dictionaries. The secret of such vitalizing
lies in the memoirs of any period. In every
generation one or two sensitive persons, with a
gift of literary power, wrote their impressions
and recollections : these books are invaluable,
because they reveal to us the conditions in
which the masters made their music. In many

359

instances, the singers *were* the conditions ; for they made the audiences, and what the audiences wanted the composers supplied. Moreover, such artists as these singers are acknowledged by men in arts other than music to have been a force modifying their work : Browning, Coleridge, Whitman, and many smaller poets, have stated their indebtedness ; and so it is well for us to respect the singers, and to see their littlenesses and deficiencies in just proportion.

Let us observe our own experiences of the singers and composers of to-day, so that at the end of our life we may write like Whitman in his seventy-second year :

Seems to me now when I look back, the Italian contralto Marietta Alboni (she is living yet, in Paris, 1891, in good condition, good voice yet, considering) with the then prominent histrions Booth, Edwin Forrest, and Fanny Kemble and the Italian singer Bettini, have had the deepest and most lasting effect upon me. I should like well if Madame Alboni and the old composer Verdi (and Bettini the tenor, if he is living) could know how much noble pleasure and happiness they gave me, and how deeply I always remember them and thank them to this day. For theatricals in literature and doubtless upon me personally, including opera, have been of course serious factors. (The experts and musicians of my present

CONCLUSION

friends claim that the new Wagner and his pieces belong far more truly to me, and I to them, likely. But I was fed and bred under the Italian dispensation, and absorb'd it, and doubtless show it.)

And finally, if we are ourselves singers, let us observe that Whitman offers thanks for *noble* pleasure and happiness given him, and see that we work to give the same.

July–August, 1924

INDEX

363

INDEX

364

INDEX

365